T0065274

THE RIGHTEOUS BRANCH

Pastor Charles Lucky Ngerem

authorHOUSE®

AuthorHouse™ UK
1663 Liberty Drive
Bloomington, IN 47403 USA
www.authorhouse.co.uk
Phone: 0800.197.4150

© 2016 Pastor Charles Lucky Ngerem. All rights reserved.

No part of this book may be reproduced, stored in a retrieval system, or transmitted by any means without the written permission of the author.

Published by AuthorHouse 02/18/2016

ISBN: 978-1-5049-9768-3 (sc)
ISBN: 978-1-5049-9769-0 (hc)
ISBN: 978-1-5049-9770-6 (e)

Print information available on the last page.

Any people depicted in stock imagery provided by Thinkstock are models, and such images are being used for illustrative purposes only. Certain stock imagery © Thinkstock.

This book is printed on acid-free paper.

Because of the dynamic nature of the Internet, any web addresses or links contained in this book may have changed since publication and may no longer be valid. The views expressed in this work are solely those of the author and do not necessarily reflect the views of the publisher, and the publisher hereby disclaims any responsibility for them.

Scripture quotations marked KJV are from the Holy Bible, King James Version (Authorized Version). First published in 1611. Quoted from the KJV Classic Reference Bible, Copyright © 1983 by The Zondervan Corporation.

Scripture quotations marked NKJV are taken from the New King James Version. Copyright © 1982 by Thomas Nelson, Inc. Used by permission. All rights reserved.

ACKNOWLEDGEMENT

I want to appreciate the almighty God who held captivity captive and released his gift upon his servant.

Thank you Rabonni for your overflowing grace and power of spirit poured upon my life.

Honour, power and dominion be unto thee forever. Amen.

It is my sincere gratitude to acknowledge my wonderful family for their immense contribution towards the success of this book. It was a team work, their moral and spiritual support made this book triumph.

I want to say a big thank you to my beloved wife Anthonia Ngerem, my potential lovely children, Michael, Oliseh, Chioma, Amaka, Brakemi and my little boy Golden. I also want to acknowledge my immediate senior brother Oliver Ngerem, my dealy sisters; Emelda, Euginia, oluchi and my good brother Kingsley Ibekwe for their great support, God will reward them

DEDICATION

I dedicate this book to my smart boy Master Golden Ngerem who has kept me warm embrace all through the creation of this book. May he remain blessed.

FOREWORD

The righteous branch is an engraved word of God which speaks of three unified cardinal points of life, the resurrection, the restitution and the rapture. It is an open revelation of the true life of the worldly man who gave himself to the will of devil. It spoke at large of how devil deceived man from the reality of life into the belief of vanity and empty glory of the earth. The spirit of God spoke expressly, that there is a magic influence upon the world, a dark shield covering the inner vision of the natural man, thereby making his sight myopic of the vision of eternal glory. The spiritual insight of the word of God has revealed that when the glorious light shall come, then there shall be a fall away of the weak. Those things that are shaking shall be removed and the perfect shall remain, the man of perdition shall be revealed, there shall be no hiding place for the disobedience of God.

The righteous branch explores on the exceeding love of Christ to the world. Why he redeemed man from his pathetic state. It elaborated what man should do to inherit the kingdom of God. Also man's allegiance to Christ for the price of his death on the Calvary.

PROLOGUE

Dear brethren, our lords harvest is ripe, your expectation to be the chosen of the lord shall not be cut off. Hold steadfast your faith in the spirit of the lord. The key word to life is salvation of soul, sanctification of spirit and belief of truth. Procrastination to the kingdom of God is the devils weapon; the power of repentance comes from the word of light, determination is a perfect step to climb the ladder that goes to heaven. Go through your wilderness in faithfulness and in your patience possess your soul.

Brethren work out your salvation with fear and trembling our God is a consuming fire to the children of disobedience.

Believe in the elect, the chosen one of God, the stone of stumbling and rock of offence, surely you will not be confounded. Stand up for the Lord Jesus Christ, be a soldier of the cross of his salvation, Trust and obey, lift up his royal banner in the faith of victory. Surely your vessel shall spring forth as a bright light that never go dim and your anointing shall be fresh oil that shall come in seven folds and shall run over.

THE MYSTERY OF THE ANCIENT OF DAYS KINGDOM

DANIEL7:9, 13,22

I BEHELD TILL THE THRONES WHERE CAST DOWN AND THE ANCIENT OF DAYS DID SEAT, WHOSE GARMENT WAS AS WHITE AS SNOW, AND THE HAIR OF HIS HEAD LIKE THE PURE WOOL: HIS THRONE WAS LIKE THE FIERY FLAME AND HIS WHEELS AS BURNING FIRE.

I SAW IN THE NIGHT VISIONS, AND, BEHOLD, ONE LIKE THE SON OF MAN CAME WITH THE CLOUDS OF HEAVEN, AND CAME TO THE ANCIENT OF DAYS, AND THEY BROUGHT HIM NEAR BEFORE HIM.

UNTIL THE ANCIENT OF DAYS CAME AND JUDGEMENT WAS GIVEN TO THE SAINTS OF THE MOST HIGH; AND THE TIME CAME THAT THE SAINTS POSSESSED THE KINGDOM.

Ancient of days kingdom is a historical divine foundation. It is the ancient spiritual bedrock; abinitio of the spirit and power, the supernatural three pillar family foundation ever existed in heaven and on earth. The ancient of days is the eternal rock of ages, the unshakable foundation of the omnipotent, omniscience and omnipresence power of the living soul. By his name "ELOHIM" he creates and recreates, and he is the deity and authority of eternal creation. This is the ancient mystery foundation, the

God in three entities with the title name engraved as of a signet. "The Holy Trinity" which stands for three names in one God. God The Father, God The Son and God The Holy Spirit. The Holy Trinity is three in one indivisible God, as the egg of a fowl is in three layers but created in one inseparable nature, that is a simple illustration of the immortal God of trinity. It is an eternal family bond of ancient stronghold which can never be broken. In divine revelation, the title names of the Holy Trinity has been revealed as Jehovah Olam, the everlasting God head, Jesus Christ Olam, the everlasting incarnate Son of God, and Holy Spirit Olam, the everlasting ancient foundation spirit divine. The reality of ancient of days is the impact of the visibility of his awesome creation, the rise of the sun and the setting of the sun, the appearance of the moon and stars in their time and season, the sea and the rivers that does not overflow their boundaries but flow through their course into their bases and the air that never seize to exist. The ancient of days is an oracle of mystery of manifestation of the spirit and power, in fire of anointing, in chariot of grace, in diverse auction of ministration and revelations. It could be through dreams, visions, prophesies, tongues or utterance, it could also be in dimension of physical appearance, mainly when conveying messages to human kind. It was by power of manifestation that Christ the Son of God was born in the world. The ancient of days is a magnificent supreme God, worthy to be praised, adore and honour because of his magnitude, power of his beauty, glory and his sovereign nature. The foundation, of ancient of days is immutable, unchangeable God who remains the same yesterday, today and forever.

1 JOHN 5:7

FOR THERE ARE THREE THAT BEAR RECORD IN HEAVEN, THE FATHER, THE WORD, AND THE HOLY GHOST: AND THESE THREE ARE ONE.

PROVERB 8:22, 23, 27, 30

THE LORD POSSESSED ME AT THE BEGINNING OF HIS WAY, BEFORE HIS WORKS OF OLD.

I HAVE BEEN ESTABLISHED FROM EVERLASTING, FROM THE BEGINNING, BEFORE THERE WAS EVER AN EARTH.

WHEN HE PREPARED THE HEAVENS, I WAS THERE WHEN HE DREW A CIRCLE ON THE FACE OF THE DEEP,

THEN I WAS BESIDE HIM AS A MASTER CRAFTSMAN; AND I WAS DAILY HIS DELIGHT, REJOICING ALWAYS BEFORE HIM.

Ancient of days is a divine foundation of royal kingdom, the kingdom above kingdoms, the high throne of all royal kingdoms, and the heaven on high called the divine heaven. Divine heaven is ruled by the law of standard and divine attributes, in quote, the law of uprightness which includes holiness, perfection, righteousness, faithfulness, love, goodness, mercy, justice and truth? Obedience is the tradition of the kingdom and the price of obedience in divine heaven are honour, peace and glory in the land of the living.

ROMANS 2:9-11

TRIBULATION AND ANGUISH, ON EVERY SOUL OF MAN WHO DOES EVIL, OF THE JEW FIRST AND ALSO OF THE GREEK;

BUT GLORY, HONOUR, AND PEACE TO EVERYONE WHO WORKS WHAT IS GOOD, TO THE JEW FIRST AND ALSO TO THE GREEK. FOR THERE IS NO PARTIALITY WITH GOD.

Ancient of days is the almighty God of heaven and earth. He is infinite in nature and awesome in reverence. He is known by his wondrous works and powerful names. "JAH" by this name, he rides in heaven, Elelyon, the most high God, Adonai, the sovereign God, Saboath the lord of host.

3

The Jews call God the father Yahweh and God the son Yashua, while the gentiles call God the father Jehovah and the son Jesus Christ.

The name Jesus Christ as a gentile name has in it a manifestation of power and dominion because it is associated with light, why, because he brought the power of light to the gentiles that broke the yoke of darkness, the name Jesus Christ remains light and power forever. The divine heaven is an eternal kingdom of illumination, the glorious immortal foundation of light. No spot of darkness neither night is found in the kingdom, evil is forbidden in the glorious kingdom of light. Every work of evil is made manifest in the marvellous light of our God. Lucifer the son of the morning, the anointed cherub, the one that work in the mid of stones of fire, these were his glorious names when he was in heaven. Notwithstanding, he was cast down in nakedness and shame with the angels that rebelled against God because evil was found in them. Ancient of days is the foundation of power, glory and faith, fear and unbelief does not exist in it. Divine heaven is not a place of sorrow, death, sickness or hunger but it is formed in righteousness, peace and joy in the Holy Spirit.

ROMANS 14:17

FOR THE KINGDOM OF GOD IS NOT MEAT AND DRINK; BUT RIGHTEOUSNESS, AND PEACE AND JOY IN THE HOLY SPIRIT.

REVELATION 21:4

AND GOD WILL WIPE AWAY EVERY TEAR FROM THEIR EYES; THERE SHALL BE NO MORE TEARS, NOR SORROW, NOR CRYING. THERE SHALL BE NO MORE PAIN, FOR THE FORMER THINGS HAVE PASSED AWAY.

The ancient of days is the God of multiplication and increase; he enlarged the coast of heaven by creating the host of heaven, who became an integral part of the everlasting foundation. God created unique creatures in heaven, the angels, the cherubim, the seraphim, chariot and horses in which each serve a great purpose in the kingdom of God. They are supernatural creatures with supernatural powers, ancient of days is always known with the identity of three in one, after the trinity he created the host of heaven and in third place he created yet another kingdom called the earth. Here he created human kind to represent his image; he created us in tripartite to represent his oracle as God in three in one. He also made a choice of three to reproduce his offspring on earth, Abraham, Isaac and Jacob, even in the transfiguration of Jesus Christ it was a terbanacle of three that beared witness of the meeting, Moses, Elijah and Jesus Christ himself. Because Adam and Eve faulted the foundation of the kingdom of earth, God in his infinite mercy granted us yet another opportunity to be adopted into his kingdom for everlasting life. Those who keep to his standard of righteousness shall be perfect to be adopted as children of the most high God. Now the kingdom of God becomes a race to win the crown of Jesus Christ for glory or to loose it for damnation. Those who are with Christ in this issue are called, chosen and faithful. Those who overcome shall be the saints of the lord and those who died in the cause of his righteousness are called the martyres of Jesus Christ. In patience shall the obedient children possess their soul in the everlasting kingdom.

REVELATION 17:6

AND I SAW THE WOMAN DRUNKEN WITH THE BLOOD OF THE SAINTS, AND WITH THE BLOOD OF THE MARTYRS OF JESUS: AND WHEN I SAW HER, I WONDERED WITH GREAT ADMIRATION

THE THOUGHT OF GOD
TOWARDS MANKIND

JEREMIAH 29:11:

"FOR I KNOW THE THOUGHTS I THINK TOWARDS YOU SAITH THE LORD, THOUGHTS OF PEACE AND NOT OF EVIL, TO GIVE YOU AN EXPECTED END."

As heavens are higher than the earth, so are the thoughts of God to mankind is in the high places and of good pleasure to bring mankind to an expected end. Our lord Jesus Christ taught us a divine prayer, a prayer that opened the door of heaven and lifted mankind to a divine fulfilment.

MATTHEW 6: 9-10:

"OUR FATHER WHICH ART IN HEAVEN, HALLOWED BE THY NAME, THY KINGDOM COME, THY WILL BE DONE ON EARTH, AS IT IS IN HEAVEN."

The will of God for mankind is to accomplish his divine purpose on earth as it is heaven, which consists of Glory, honour and peace in the land of the living. God loves us from the foundation of the world, and desire us to be an integral part of his kingdom. He wants our willingness and obedience to follow in the truth of his ways, which by faith and long patience will bring man to a fruitful end. Our creator expects us to follow him as a congregation of sheep with a caring shepherd, who will lead his sheep to a green pasture. With trust and confidence in the God of hope, we shall eat the good of the land, if we keep our ways steadfast in the spirit of the lord, and also be truthful to his words.

ISAIAH 1: 18-20:

"COME NOW AND LET US REASON TOGETHER, SAID THE LORD, THOUGH YOUR SINS BE AS SCARLET, THEY SHALL BE AS WHITE AS SNOW, THOUGH THEY BE RED LIKE CRIMSON, THEY SHALL BE AS WOOL, IF YE BE WILLING AND OBEDIENT, YE SHALL EAT THE GOOD OF THE LAND, BUT IF YE REFUSE AND REBEL, YE SHALL BE DEVOURED WITH THE SWORD, FOR THE MOUTH OF THE LORD HAS SPOKEN IT."

Adam and Eve sinned against God and was cast away from God's presence, but still God has a treasure in man that he cannot let go, the treasure of his glory and of his image which he cannot share with any other God. For this reason, God trail through this part to rediscover man and his missing treasure which shows a replica of him in the mirror of God.

God carefully looked into the heart of man and saw a heavenly manifestation in the son of lamech, Noah who he decisively used to rediscover man to continue in the expedition of life and expected end. Our creator always look forward to see man repent of his evil ways and have a divine attitude in the spirit, that is exactly what fascinated God in the son of Jared, Enoch and Noah the son of lamech that through them he established yet another relationship with man. Though they were in the evil generation but their hearts and actions served God in the beauty of his holiness. God having established a covenant with Noah not to destroy man by flood again desired a more convenient covenant to bring man to his expected end. To this end, his heart went in search of a man of faith, patience and courage who could bring the covenant to a fulfilment. That man came to be Abraham the son of Terah who truly God used to establish his covenant of promises and blessings to the children of God today, to the Jews and the gentiles.

GALATIANS 3:14:

"THAT THE BLESSINGS OF ABRAHAM MIGHT COME TO THE GENTILES THROUGH JESUS CHRIST, THAT WE MIGHT RECEIVE THE PROMISES OF THE SPIRIT THROUGH FAITH.

The agape love of God for mankind from the foundation of the world propelled his action to continue the search to bring man to his expected end. The quest to discover a man of divine attribute directed his attention to the family of Jesse. And in this case, David became the chosen one to bear the fruit of the expected end. Through this blessed lineage of David, the first fruit of the expected end, the son of God was born through the root of Jesse according to the word of God. Jesus Christ of Nazareth the first fruit of the kingdom became the sacrificial lamb to shed his blood to redeem man from the age of darkness to the age of light. He became the way, the truth and life to them that believe in him. He is the door by which the living in him goes through to the kingdom of God. Today the spirit of the living God bears witness with the spirit of all believers in this end time that we are children of God by faith in the blood of Jesus. This is our expected end from God to live an eternal life which became true through Jesus Christ of Nazareth.

ISAIAH 11:1-2,

"AND THERE SHALL COME FORTH A ROD OUT OF THE STEM OF JESSE, AND A BRANCH SHALL GROW OUT OF HIS ROOTS.

AND THE SPIRIT OF THE LORD SHALL REST UPON HIM, THE SPIRIT OF WISDOM AND UNDERSTANDING, THE SPIRIT OF COUNSEL AND MIGHT, THE SPIRIT OF KNOWLEDGE AND OF THE FEAR OF THE LORD.

The entrance of his birth made way for our rebirth as born again children of God, his death destroyed our flesh on the Calvary which is irrelevant in the kingdom of God and his risen from death gave us a glorious ascension to heaven as children of the kingdom.

The good tiding of God to man is to achieve heaven through Jesus his son by willingness and obedience, but not without tribulation and long suffering, though the end of hope and faith in Christ is glory.

REVELATION 7:13-15:

"AND ONE OF THE ELDERS ANSWERED SAYING UNTO ME, WHAT ARE THESE WHICH ARE ARRAYED IN WHITE ROBES? AND WHENCE CAME THEY?

AND I SAID UNTO HIM, SIR THOU KNOWEST. AND HE SAID TO ME, THESE ARE THEY WHICH CAME OUT OF GREAT TRIBULATION, AND HAVE WASHED THEIR ROBES, AND MADE THEM WHITE IN THE BLOOD OF THE LAMB.

THE GLAD TIDING BEARER

ISAIAH 40:9:

O ZION, THAT BRINGEST GOOD TIDINGS, GET THEE UP INTO THE HIGH MOUNTAIN; O JERUSALEM, THAT BRINGEST GOOD TIDINGS, LIFT UP THY VOICE WITH STRENGTH, LIFT IT UP, BE NOT AFRAID; SAY UNTO THE CITIES OF JUDAH, BEHOLD YOUR GOD!

The book of prophet Isaiah said "who had believed our report? And to whom is the arm of the lord revealed" Among the prophets that God sent to the earth every one spoke according to the word given to him by the spirit of God, but the exception amongst them is the son of God, the prophet who came from heaven, the only messenger of God who knows the arm of God. Jesus Christ the son of God is the glad tiding bearer, the only messenger that brought peculiar news of the divine kingdom of his father to the people of the earth. Christ is the word of his father, the peculiar word of the Alpha and Omega and the Amen. By divine virtue he became the bearer of the word, the announcer, the town crier and the tale bearer of the kingdom of his father. The word of the scroll he beared in his hands spoke about himself and the kingdom of his father, the word of salvation and eternal life, the word of light and power that broke the yoke of darkness. The world did not receive his word because his word spoke of the iniquity of the world. But to them that God revealed the light of the word, also receive the spirit of the word and it becomes a glad tiding and salvation to their souls.

ROMANS 10:15:

AND HOW SHALL THEY PREACH, EXCEPT THEY BE SENT? AS IT IS WRITTEN, HOW BEAUTIFUL ARE THE FEET OF THEM THAT PREACH THE GOSPEL OF PEACE, AND BRING GLAD TIDINGS OF GOOD THINGS.

Christ as the bearer of the word did not speak of his own word but the word of he who has sent him. He did not act on his own authority but the authority of his father. He was the ambassador of the word of his father, master, the Raboni of the word which he spoke in power of knowledge and wisdom. All along his dwelling in the world his father did not desert him but dwelled in him as he was in his father, everything he did was by his father's approval as his father glorified his good works.

JOHN 14:10:

BELIEVEST THOU NOT THAT I AM IN THE FATHER, AND THE FATHER IN ME? THE WORDS THAT I SPEAK UNTO YOU I SPEAK NOT OF MYSELF: BUT THE FATHER THAT DWELLETH IN ME, HE DOETH THE WORKS.

He spoke according to the will of his father, and his word was the word of power and of the spirit. Nothing has he said out of his mouth that was not spoken through the utterance of the spirit. The spirit ordained him in all things of good manners; his word was of wisdom and truth and was spoken in no measure. He came not to condemn the world but to rebuke and reproof the world of their iniquity, his mission was not to destroy the law of the prophets but to accomplish it. His word was not the word of peace to the people on earth but sword to put division between evil and good. All things are delivered to him by his father even the authority to reveal who the father is.

MATHEW 11:27:

ALL THINGS ARE DELIVERED UNTO ME OF MY FATHER: AND NO MAN KNOWETH THE SON, BUT THE FATHER; NEITHER KNOWETH ANY MAN THE FATHER, SAVE THE SON, AND HE TO WHOMSOEVER THE SON WILL REVEAL HIM.

The power of death and risen is in his hands according to his father's authority. His calling is a sacrifice of death that will raise men unto his father according to his father's will that men should have eternal life and become the heir to his throne.

JOHN 6:39:

AND THIS IS THE FATHER'S WILL WHICH HATH SENT ME, THAT OF ALL WHICH HE HATH GIVEN ME I SHOULD LOOSE NOTHING, BUT SHOULD RAISE IT UP AGAIN AT THE LAST DAY.

A STAR IN A MANGER

NUMBERS 24:17

I SHALL SEE HIM, BUT NOT NOW, I SHALL BEHOLD HIM, BUT NOT NIGH: THERE SHALL COME A STAR OUT OF JACOB, AND A SCEPTRE SHALL RISE OUT OF ISRAEL AND SHALL SMITE THE CORNERS OF MOAB AND DESTROY ALL THE CHILDREN OF SHETH.

A star is born and not made, a star is not assessed by quality of intelligence or dynamism but it is an inscription in the placenta of birth and a charisma in the face. Jesus Christ was born to be a child of destiny, a star deep in the blood, a baby of the Holy Spirit. He was conceived of the Holy Spirit and carried in the womb of a virgin mother chosen by God and parented by a man chosen by God who has not known a woman. In this sense this attributes is traced to be a divine gift and that confirms him as a baby with a star of purpose. His star being prophesied by holy men of God is another sign of divine identity that made his star supernatural. The star of Jesus rose from the east where the sun rises from each day, he was born in the eastern part of the world, the Middle East. And in the city of Judea his nativity, his birth took place in the eastern part of the town called Bethlehem. This symbolises his being a child of Light, no wonder he is called the bright and morning star.

According to the word of God the eyes of the three shepherds in the field was opened to see the glorious star of Jesus Christ. The story said that his star moved from its orbit directing them to the place where the baby was born, as they followed the direction of the star they came to a town called Bethlehem in Judea and in this place they found a new born baby wrapped in swaddling clothes and kept in a manger in the sheep fold. The environmental circumstance of his birth depicts another significant meaning to his star of purpose. His birth taking place in the sheep fold and in a manger is not by accident but a destiny to manifest the purpose of his calling, for every of God's action there is a wisdom attached. Jesus Christ being born in a poor environment means that he is called for the poor and humble, for the wounded, for the broken hearted, for those who are in captivity and to lead the sheep of God which is the contents of the manifest of the seven seals. His mission is to lift up the poor and the lofty to be abased.

ISAIAH 26:5-6

FOR HE BRINGETH DOWN THEM THAT DWELL ON HIGH, THE LOFTY CITY, HE LAYETH IT LOW, HE LAYETH IT LOW,EVEN TO THE GROUND; HE BRINGETH IT EVEN TO THE DUST.

THE FOOT SHALL TREAD IT DOWN, EVEN THE FEET OF THE POOR, AND THE STEPS OF THE NEEDY.

Owing the fact that he is a star of purpose, the killers of the divine star came against him to destroy his star of mission. King Herod of Jerusalem rose against the baby Jesus to destroy him but because he was born by grace and live by grace that God made a way of escape for him. It was for the reason of destroying him that all the children in Ramah was killed. The hands of God was upon him until the very day he declared open his mission on earth in the temple of God in his home town Nazareth. That day the world bore witness of his exceeding riches in wisdom as he read the book of Isaiah 60:1-3.

THE TREES OF EDEN

EZEKIEL 7:10-11

BEHOLD THE DAY, BEHOLD, IT IS COME: THE MORNING IS COME FORTH; THE ROD HATH BLOSSOMED, PRIDE HAD BUDDED. VIOLENCE IS RISEN UP INTO A ROD OF WICKEDNESS: NONE OF THEM SHALL REMAIN, NOR OF THEIR MULTITUDE, NOR ANY OF THEIRS: NEITHER SHALL THERE BE WAILING FOR THEM.

Ego and pride goes before a fall. The love of the world is lust of the flesh, lust of the eyes and pride of life. The trees of Eden were planted in righteousness and in the glory of God but when the serpent crept into its branches it defiled the stems and polluted the fruits and made them sour. This is the issue of man in the paradise of God the Garden of Eden. God created him in his image and in his glory and hoped in him to receive his glorification but rather he followed after the wisdom of error which led him to disobey his creator and in his conceit he became accursed. In the same vein today, God has planted many in his royal vineyard hoping to reap their fruit but many has grown wild and become thorns and briers and produce the fruit of tares. God has sworn to cut them down if they do not repent and come back to him, they will remain under a curse of damnation and will be a stubble. God has called us a call of blessing and not of wrath but when we disobey him and follow after the spirit of error the fellow becomes accursed and his story will be like a tale that is told by the old prophets.

PASLM 90:8-9

THOU HAST SET OUR INIQUITIES BEFORE THEE, OUR SECRET SINS IN THE LIGHT OF THY COUNTENANCE. FOR ALL OUR DAYS ARE PASSED AWAY IN THY WRATH: WE SPEND OUR YEARS AS A TALE THAT IS TOLD.

There is no ignorance in the sheep fold of God. Every sheep dwell in the light of the Lord and receive spiritual insight from the spirit of God. So if the spirit of man is misled it therefore means he was not submissive to the control of the Holy Spirit and apparently something contrary has occupied his vessel. A child of God who is sealed by the Holy Spirit redemption is supposed to be under the control of the Holy Spirit, influenced and monitored. A vessel who refuse to listen to God's instruction is not worthy to be called the sheep of God but a stubborn goat destined to fall into the pit of hell. Adam and Eve fell into the trap of spiritual death because of negligence of the word of God. Nebuchadnezzar glorified himself because of ego and pride, Pharaoh was stone hearted because of the rod of wickedness in him. Ahab and Jezebel died because of the spirit of covetousness, and this are the devices of the devil. Dear brethren be careful what you wish for, God is a consuming fire, the avenger of his enemies. Every tree that does not bear the fruit of righteousness in the vineyard of God shall be cut down and be trodden under feet.

EZEKIEL 31:18

TO WHOM ART THOU THUS LIKE A GLORY AND IN GREATNESS AMONG THE TREES OF EDEN? YET SHALT THOU BE BROUGHT DOWN WITH THE TREES OF EDEN UNTO THE NETHER PARTS OF EARTH: THOU SHALT LIE IN THE MIDST OF THE UNCIRCUMCISED WITH THEM THAT BE SLAIN BY THE SWORD. THIS IS PHARAOH AND ALL HIS MULTITUDE, SAITH THE LORD GOD.

BREAK UP THE FALLOW GROUND

ZECHARIAH 12:10

AND I WILL POUR UPON THE HOUSE OF DAVID, AND UPON THE INHABITANTS OF JERUSALEM, THE SPIRIT OF GRACE AND OF SUPPLICATION: AND THEY SHALL LOOK UPON ME WHOM THEY HAVE PIERCED, AND THEY SHALL MOURN FOR HIM, AS ONE MOURNETH FOR HIS ONLY SON, AND SHALL BE IN BITTERNESS FOR HIM, AS ONE THAT IS IN BITTERNESS FOR HIS FIRST BORN.

Daughters of sorceress till your stone hearted ground that the seed of Christ will grow thereof. Sons of Jezebel, the seat of devil, yield a repentant heart meet to receive the light of Christ. You counsel of Belial, do not be hard hearted but incline your heart to wisdom, surrender your fallow ground to the great sower to sow in you a seed of eternal life. Jesus Christ is a sower looking for a fallow ground to sow his precious seed. Is your heart available for him? The earth is the Lord's and fullness thereof, Christ created mankind and his fallow ground. He is justice gracious, his sincere offer is that the man he has created will surrender his fallow ground in obedience and willingness. It is our father's pleasure to cast away our transgressions, give us a new heart and renew a right spirit within us. Wisdom will defeat the enemy, had I known is a later word left with no option. Arise now and shine the light of Christ has come upon you, make way that darkness be overcome and be clothed in the glory of God.

HOSEA 10:12-13

SOW TO YOURSELVES IN RIGHTEOUSNESS, REAP IN MERCY; BREAK UP YOUR FALLOW GROUND: FOR IT IS TIME TO SEEK THE LORD, TILL HE COME AND RAIN RIGHTEOUNESS UPON YOU. YE HAVE PLOUGHED WICKEDNESS, YE HAVE REAPED INIQUITY; YE HAVE EATEN THE FRUIT OF LIES: BECAUSE THOU DIDST TRUST IN THY WAY, IN THE MULTITUDE OF THY MIGHTY MEN.

Wake up from slumber of spiritual death, Christ offered himself for sacrifice to redeem you from the power of death. He died for your ungodliness, your adultery, your fornication, your robbery and all manners of iniquity in this world. His death was a subject of oppression and affliction but it pleased his father that he was bruised, smitten, rejected and despised by men only to reconcile us with his father. Why does your heart wax gross, your ears dull of hearing to receive the Holy Ghost advances of redemption.

ACTS 28:27-28

FOR THE HEART OF THIS PEOPLE IS WAXED GROSS, AND THEIR EARS ARE DULL OF HEARING, AND THEIR EYES HAVE THEY CLOSED; LEST THEY SHOULD SEE WITH THEIR EYES, AND SEE WITH THEIR EARS, AND UNDERSTAND WITH THEIR HEART, AND SHOULD BE CONVERTED, AND I SHOULD HEAL THEM. BE IT KNOWN THEREFORE UNTO YOU, THAT THE SALVATION OF GOD IS SENT UNTO THE GENTILES, AND THAT THEY WILL HEAR IT.

Blessed are they that receive the spirit of the Lord and his truth, the light of God and salvation has come unto them as rock. Truly they seek and have found.

ISAIAH 55:6-7:

SEEK YE THE LORD WHILE HE MAY BE FOUND, CALL UPON HIM WHILE HE IS NEAR: LET THE WICKED FORSAKE HIS WAY, AND THE UNRIGHTEOUS MAN HIS THOUGHTS: AND LET HIM RETURN UNTO THE LORD, AND HE WILL HAVE MERCY UPON HIM; AND TO OUR GOD, FOR HE WILL ABUNDANTLY PARDON.

THE LION OF THE TRIBE OF JUDAH PREVAILED

LUKE 4:17-20

AND THERE WAS DELIVERED UNTO HIM THE BOOK OF THE PROPHET ESAIAS. AND WHEN HE HAD OPENED THE BOOK, HE FOUND THE PLACE WHERE IT WAS WRITTEN, THE SPIRIT OF THE LORD IS UPON ME, BECAUSE HE HATH ANOINTED ME TO PREACH THE GOSPEL TO THE POOR; HE HATH SENT ME TO HEAL THE BROKENHEARTED, TO PREACH DELIVERANCE TO THE CAPTIVES, AND RECOVERING OF SIGHT TO THE BLIND, TO SET AT LIBERTY THEM THAT ARE BRUISE, TO PREACH THE ACCEPTABLE YEAR OF THE LORD.

AND HE CLOSED THE BOOK, AND HE GAVE IT BACK TO THE MINISTER, AND SAT DOWN. AND THE EYES OF ALL THEM THAT WERE IN THE SYNAGOGUE WERE FASTENED ON HIM.

According to the word of God in the vision of John the servant of our Lord Jesus Christ, the book of revelation said there was a great question in heaven that needed a perfect answer and the question says "Who is worthy to open the book and to lose the seven seals thereof?" The bible also made it clear that there was a great silence in heaven, no man in heaven, nor in earth, neither under the earth was able to open the book neither to look thereof. But John still in trance in a vision saw in the midst of the throne and of the four beast, and in the midst of the elders stood a lamb as it had been slain, having seven horns and seven eyes, which are the seven spirits of God sent forth into the earth. And abruptly the voice of the elders in heaven said to John "Weep not, behold the Lion of the tribe of Judah, the root of David hath prevailed to open the book and to lose the seven seals thereof. The bible recorded that there was an ovation of joy in heaven and they sang a new song. This becomes a great hope and faith to the dwellers in heaven and on earth.

The Lion of the tribe of Judah stood out among men of the earth and prevailed in an invisible battle to redeem the people of God from the ancient gates and everlasting doors of the pit of hell. Immanuel who was baptised to be Jesus Christ of Nazareth is the only man in flesh whose star is destined to have the sceptre of authority to deliver man from the power of eternal death through the power in his blood which he shed on the cross of Calvary

REVELATION 5: 9-10

AND THEY SUNG A NEW SONG, SAYING, THOU ART WORTHY TO TAKE THE BOOK, AND TO OPEN THE SEALS THEREOF FOR THOU WAST SLAIN, AND HAST REDEEMED US TO GOD BY THY BLOOD OUT OF EVERY KINDRED AND TONGUE AND PEOPLE, AND NATION.

AND HAST MADE US UNTO OUR GOD KINGS AND PRIESTS AND WE SHALL REIGN ON THE EARTH.

Certainly the power of salvation has come to this generation; the tabernacle of God is here among men, no more woe but joy to the inhabitants of the earth. Those who run into the tower of Christ are like mount Zion that can never be moved, like a horn of a unicorn that shall be exalted and anointed with fresh oil. The joy of the righteous are everlasting because they are like trees planted by the rivers of water that bring forth it's fruit in season. Rejoice o ye faithful, for Christ our Lord has overcome the world and the devil, and by his blood we have become overcomers of the enemies of Christ.

JOHN 16:33

THESE THINGS I HAVE SPOKEN UNTO YOU, THAT IN ME YE MIGHT HAVE PEACE. IN THE WORLD YE SHALL HAVE TRIBULATION: BUT BE OF GOOD CHEER; I HAVE OVERCOME THE WORLD.

Because we have believed in the truth, the light of Jesus shines upon us and we have no place in the darkness. Our light prevailed against darkness and we become children of the day and not of the night any longer. The gate of hell shall not prevail against the church of God because Jesus has firstly prevailed against it. To this intent our glorious church prevailed against the church of flesh which means our spirit prevailed against the flesh, the world and the devil.

ROMANS 7:6

BUT NOW WE ARE DELIVERED FROM THE LAW, THAT BEING DEAD WHEREIN WE WERE HELD; THAT WE SHOULD SERVE IN NEWNESS OF SPIRIT AND NOT IN THE OLDNESS OF THE LETTER.

CHRIST LEADS

EXODUS 13:20-21

SO THEY TOOK THEIR JOURNEY FROM SUC'COTH AND CAMPED IN E'THAM AT THE EDGE OF THE WILDERNESS.AND THE LORD WENT BEFORE THEM BY DAY IN A PILLAR OF CLOUD TO LEAD THE WAY AND BY NIGHT IN A PILLAR OF FIRE TO GIVE THEM LIGHT SO AS TO GO BY DAY AND NIGHT.

A man of vision sees through tomorrow and prepares for its expectations; his eyes are full of sight to lead the way. A blind man is myopic and cannot see far he is blind even in the light of the day; Jesus Christ is the leader of the fellowship of light. There has never been any prophet like him who has come in flesh in this world, who died and rose alive and ascended to his father in heaven. No religious leader ever died and buried rose and ascended to his father, Christ is the only religious leader who has fulfilled this spiritual mystery because his mission is a supernatural call to lead. Christ is an exceptional leader, a leader of the generation of light and living. He leads the fellowship of the humble heart, the Lamb of God.

The acclaimed leaders, who came behind him, came in through the back door and they are leaders of the fellowship of goats. They have come to reap where they did not sow; they are blind leaders of the blind. A blind man cannot lead the way if not both blind will fall into a ditch.

JOHN 10:1-2

MOST ASSUREDLY, I SAY TO YOU, HE WHO DOES NOT ENTER THE SHEEPFOLD BY THE DOOR, BUT CLIMBS UP SOME OTHER WAY, THE SAME IS A THEIF AND A ROBBER. BUT HE WHO ENTERS BY THE DOOR IS THE SHEPHERD OF THE SHEEP.

Christ is the way, the truth and life, he is a lamp unto our feet directing us to the way of eternal life. He is a leader in the path of righteousness.

PROVERB 8:20:

I LEAD IN THE WAY OF RIGHTEOUSNESS, IN THE MIDST OF THE PATHS OF JUDGMENT.

Christ is a shepherd, Rohi the leader of flocks of God, who give life to his flocks by leading them to graze in green pasture. He was the shepherd of his disciples and also the shepherd of the disciples of all generation.

THE 7 ROYAL DIADEM OF CHRIST

ISAIAH 28:5-6

IN THAT DAY THE LORD OF HOST WILL BE FOR A CROWN OF GLORY AND A DIADEM OF BEAUTY TO THE REMNANT OF HIS PEOPLE,

FOR A SPIRIT OF JUSTICE TO HIM WHO SITS IN JUDGEMENT, AND FOR STRENGTH TO THOSE WHO TURN BACK THE BATTLE AT THE GATE.

The seven royal diadem of Christ is the seven in one crown of Christ. It is the crown of glory, power, honour and beauty of HIS royal majesty Jesus Christ of Nazareth as the Alpha and Omega the beginning and the end of all things of heaven and earth, the Amen and Amen.

The seven crowns of Christ is governed by seven stars and seven spirits which made Jesus Christ the head of all principalities and powers.

REVELATION 3:1

"AND TO THE ANGEL OF THE CHURCH IN SARDIS WRITE, THESE THINGS SAYS HE WHO HAS THE SEVEN SPIRITS OF GOD AND THE SEVEN STARS: "I KNOW YOUR WORKS, THAT YOU HAVE A NAME THAT YOU ARE ALIVE, BUT YOU ARE DEAD.

The titles of the seven crowns are:

*The crown of the Alpha and Omega and the Amen.

*The crown of prince of life and the bishop of our soul.

*The crown of saviour and the light of the world.

*The crown of prince of peace.

*The crown of chief shepherd.

*The crown of king of kings and lord of lords.

*The crown of king of glory.

The Crown Of Alpha And The Omega And The Amen

REVELATION 1:7-8

BEHOLD, HE IS COMING WITH CLOUDS, AND EVERY EYE WILL SEE HIM, EVEN THEY WHO PIERCED HIM. AND ALL THE TRIBES OF THE EARTH WILL MOURN BECAUSE OF HIM. EVEN SO, AMEN.

"I AM THE ALPHA AND THE OMEGA, THE BEGINNING AND THE END, SAYS THE LORD, WHO IS AND WHO WAS AND WHO IS TO COME, THE ALMIGHTY.

Jesus Christ is the beginning and the end of all things of heaven and earth. By him all things were created and by him all things will come to an end. He was before all things and by him all things consist. He is the image of the invisible God, the first born over all creation. In him the fullness of all things dwell, the Alpha and the Omega and the Amen.

COLOSSIANS 1:15-17

HE IS THE IMAGE OF THE INVISIBLE GOD, THE FIRST BORN OVER ALL CREATION.

FOR BY HIM ALL THINGS WERE CREATED THAT ARE IN HEAVEN AND THAT ARE ON EARTH, VISIBLE AND INVISIBLE, WHETHER THRONES OR DOMINIONS OR PRINCIPALITIES OR POWERS. ALL THINGS WERE CREATED THROUGH HIM AND FOR HIM.

AND HE IS BEFORE ALL THINGS, AND IN HIM ALL THINGS CONSIST.

Christ is the Amen in all things. He is the word that proceeds from God's mouth that ended in amen. Christ is a seal of every word of God which is amen. Amen is a seal of accomplishment in the word of God, a final word that can never be broken.

REVELATIONS 3: 14

AND TO THE ANGELS IN THE IN THE CHURCH OF THE LAODICEANS WRITE, THESE THINGS SAYS THE AMEN, THE FAITHFUL AND THE TRUE WITNESS, THE BEGINNING OF THE CREATION OF GOD.

The Crown Of Prince Of Life And Bishop Of Our Soul.

ACTS 3: 14-15

BUT YOU DENIED THE HOLY ONE AND THE JUST, AND ASKED FOR A MUDERER TO BE GRANTED TO YOU,

"AND KILLED THE PRINCE OF LIFE WHOM GOD RAISED FROM THE DEAD, OF WHICH WE ARE WITHNESSES.

Jesus Christ is the prince of life, the source of life and the cord that sustains the breath of life, he becomes the essence of life and the reason why all living things must live. The contents of our lives are in him, he is the energy source of our life, the power that sustains the life and the power that terminate the life. The cord of our life is the spirit in us and the source is Christ. He has the power to call our spirit anytime any moment.

1 JOHN 5:12

HE WHO HAS THE SON HAS LIFE; HE WHO DOES NOT HAVE THE SON OF GOD DOES NOT HAVE LIFE.

Christ is the owner of our soul, the preserver of our soul. He is a judge to every soul. He destines our soul to its destination according to our work. The souls that work iniquity shall inherit hell, the soul that work righteousness shall inherit heaven the kingdom of God. He died to save our soul and he becomes the bishop of our soul. He wants our soul to return back to him in purity.

1 PETER 2:25

FOR YOU WERE LIKE SHEEP GOING ASTRAY, BUT ARE NOW RETURNED TO THE SHEPHERD AND BISHOP OF YOUR SOULS.

The Crown Of Saviour And Light Of The World.

LUKE 2:11-12

"FOR there IS BORN TO YOU THIS DAY IN THE CITY OF DAVID A SAVIOUR, WHO IS CHRIST THE LORD.

AND THIS WILL BE THE SIGN TO YOU: YOU WILL FIND A BABY WRAPPED IN SWADDLING CLOTHES LYING IN A MANGER.

From the foundation of the world the delight of Jesus Christ is to bring mankind to his expected end. He has a unique and perfect love for him and his call was unto men to be the heir of the throne of his father. It was out of genuine love that he gave his life a ransom to save the world from eternal death. The world was like a ship destined to sink into hell for an everlasting disaster but Jesus offered his life to float ashore the vessel of men, and he saved the souls of men who might believe in him.

1 JOHN 4:14

AND WE HAVE SEEN AND TESTIFY THAT THE FATHER HAS SENT THE SON AS THE SAVIOUR OF THE WORLD.

Christ came to the world to light up the world from its dark age to marvellous light of his divine blessings. In him is the spirit of light that light up the heart of men into understanding of the knowledge of God. The mystery of our fellowship with the Lord is in the spirit of light which separates us from the spirit of darkness and bring to wisdom the intent of principalities and powers and as well the manifold wisdom of God to our will.

JOHN 8:12

THEN JESUS SPOKE TO THEM AGAIN, SAYING, "I AM THE LIGHT OF THE WORLD, HE WHO FOLLOWS ME SHALL NOT WALK IN DARKNESS, BUT HAVE THE LIGHT OF LIFE.

The Crown Of Prince Of Peace

ISAIAH 9:6

FOR UNTO US A CHILD IS BORN, UNTO US A SON IS GIVEN; AND THE GOVERNMENT WILL BE UPON HIS SHOULDER. AND HIS NAME WILL BE CALLED WONDERFUL, COUNSELOR, MIGHTY GOD, EVERLASTING FATHER, PRINCE OF PEACE.

From the beginning peace has been the priority of God to mankind, a place of absolute peace like heaven. That becomes the reason why God created paradise an inhabitable place for man. In the beginning all creatures of the universe were in total harmony on the surface of the earth until the presence of the ancient serpent was manifested, since then sorrow took over the affairs of man and peace was no more found. Man sold his confidence and dominion over to Satan, fear and doubt was made manifest in his life. For this purpose the son of God was manifested that he might destroy the works of the devil. His desire to bring the thought of his father to our expected end, which is the thought of peace made him to offer himself a sacrifice on the Calvary to bring peace to mankind through his blood which he shed for the sake of salvation for mankind.

ISAIAH 53:5

BUT HE WAS WOUNDED FOR OUR TRANSGRESSIONS, HE WAS BRUISED FOR OUR INIQUITIES; THE CHASTISEMENT OF OUR PEACE WAS UPON HIM, AND BY HIS STRIPES WE ARE HEALED.

The Crown Of Chief Shepherd

1 PETER 5:2-4.

SHEPHERD THE FLOCKS OF GOD WHICH IS AMONG YOU, SERVING AS OVERSEERS, NOT

BY COMPULSION BUT WILLINGLY, NOT FOR DISHONEST GAIN BUT EAGERLY;

NOR AS BEING LORDS OVER THOSE ENTRUSTED TO YOU, BUT BEING EXAMPLE OF THE FLOCK;

AND WHEN THE CHIEF SHEPHERD APPEARS, YOU WILL RECEIVE CROWN OF GLORY THAT DOES NOT FADE AWAY.

The major purpose why Jesus Christ manifested on earth is to look for the scattered flocks of God and to gather them into his fellowship. In the beginning, man has gone astray in his own way and has no shepherd until Jesus came to the world and made his call unto men of the world. He has demanded that they come out of their evil ways and follow the good shepherd, so as to graze on a good pasture and as well rest their soul in the land of the living. He died for this sake, to draw men unto himself.

Christ came for the lost sheep, those who are lost in the cloud of darkness. His voice today is calling out for the lost sheep to come out from the shadow of death and come unto him, the good shepherd. Rohi the chief shepherd has promised that He will not rest until he has gathered his people to himself.

EZEKIEL 34:11-14

"FOR THUS SAYS THE LORD GOD: "INDEED I MYSELF WILL SEARCH FOR MY SHEEP, AND SEEK THEM OUT.

"AS A SHEPHERD SEEKS OUT HIS FLOCK ON THE DAY HE IS AMONG HIS SCATTERED SHEEP, SO WILL I SEEK OUT MY SHEEP AND DELIVER THEM FROM ALL THE PLACES WHERE THEY WERE SCATTERED ON A CLOUDY AND DARK DAY.

"AND I WILL BRING THEM OUT FROM THE PEOPLE, AND GATHER THEM FROM THE

COUNTRIES, AND WILL BRING THEM TO THEIR OWN LAND; I WILL FEED THEM ON THE MOUNTAINS OF ISRAEL, IN THE VALLEYS AND IN THE INHABITED PLACES OF THE COUNTRY.

The Crown Of King Of Kings And Lord Of Lords

1 TIMOTHY 6:14-15

THAT YOU KEEP THIS COMMANDMENT WITHOUT SPOT, BLAMELESS UNTIL OUR LORD JESUS CHRIST APPEARING, WHICH HE WILL MANIFEST, HE WHO IS THE BLESSED AND ONLY POTENTATE, THE KING OF KINGS AND LORD OF LORDS.

Jesus Christ of Nazareth is from the eternal foundation of the royal kingdom, the first born in the divine home of kings and princes. His kingship is possessed from the everlasting foundation as the king of all that existed. The staff and sceptre of royal kingship is his authority. Christ crown kings and princes and give them the authority to decree justice'

In Jerusalem the city of kings, Christ rode on a tender colt celebrating his kingship as the king of kings and lord of lords of all things above and on earth.

On that day there was no controversy over his kingship and his lordship. The world witnessed and acknowledged his authority which he lorded over every king and prince of the earth. Even Pontius Pilate justified this when he asked Jesus a question "Art thou the king of the Jews? And he answered him and said Thou sayest it".

REVELATION 1:5-6

AND FROM JESUS CHRIST THE FAITHFUL WITNESS, THE FIRSTBORN FROM THE DEAD, AND THE RULER OVER THE KINGS OF THE

EARTH. TO HIM WHO LOVED US AND WASHED US FROM OUR SINS IN HIS OWN BLOOD.

AND HAS MADE US KINGS AND PRIESTS TO HIS GOD AND FATHER, TO HIM BE GLORY AND DOMINION FOR EVER AND EVER. AMEN.

The earth is the Lord's and the fullness thereof, the world and they that dwell therein. There are many gods and many lords both on earth and in heaven but we know only but one Lord, Jesus Christ the supreme of all lords.

REVELATION 19:15-16

NOW OUT OF HIS MOUTH GOES A SHARP SWORD, THAT WITH IT HE SHOULD STRIKE THE NATIONS. AND HE HIMSELF WILL RULE THEM WITH A ROD OF IRON. HE HIMSELF TREADS THE WINEPRESS OF THE FIERCENESS AND WRATH OF ALMIGHTY GOD.

AND HE HAS ON HIS ROBE AND ON HIS THIGH A NAME WRITTEN:

KING OF KINGS
AND LORD OF LORDS.

The Crown Of King Of Glory

PSALM 24:7-10

LIFT UP YOUR HEADS, O YOU GATES AND BE LIFTED UP, YOU EVERLASTING DOORS! AND THE KING OF GLORY SHALL COME IN.

WHO IS THIS KING OF GLORY? THE LORD STRONG AND MIGHTY, THE LORD MIGHTY IN BATTLE.

LIFT UP YOUR HEADS, O YOU GATES! LIFT UP, YOU EVERLASTING DOORS! AND THE KING OF GLORY SHALL COME IN.

WHO IS THIS KING OF GLORY? THE LORD OF HOSTS, HE IS THE KING OF GLORY.

The glory of Christ is from the eternal foundation of the spirit of glory. The glory of Jesus is his fame, his majesty his magnitude, his praises, his honour, and his awesomeness. Jesus Christ belongs to the royal family of the glory of God and the spirit of glory is in him. He is the first on earth to receive the spirit of glory. On the day of his immersion baptism the spirit of glory fell upon him. Christ is the deity of glory, that's why he is the lord of host of the crown of glory.

His birth was glorious because he was conceived of the holy spirit of glory and his death was glorious because his father and the Holy Spirit glorified him before death. His resurrection was glorious because the Holy spirit lived in him and quickened him to ascend in glory to his father. In conclusion he is the God head of glory, the crown head of all glory.

PSALM 148:13

LET THEM PRAISE THE NAME OF THE LORD, FOR HIS NAME ALONE IS EXALTED; HIS GLORY IS ABOVE THE EARTH AND HEAVEN.

THE 4 SQUARE IN THE BODY OF CHRIST

There are four divisions of transformation in the body of Christ. Its necessity is to form the tripartite of the believer's body, the body, the soul and spirit to an immortal entity.

The four divisions are:

*Purification of body and quickening of the spirit

*Eating the body of Christ and drinking of his blood

*The burden of the cross.

*The reward of crown.

Purification Of Body And Quickening Of The Spirit

ROMANS 6:4

THEREFORE WE WERE BURIED WITH HIM THROUGH BAPTISM INTO DEATH, THAT JUST AS CHRIST WAS RAISED FROM THE DEAD BY THE GLORY OF THE FATHER, EVEN SO WE ALSO SHOULD WALK IN NEWNESS OF LIFE.

This is the first stage of transformation in the body of Christ; it is called the baptismal and the redemption stage. The transformation here is the removal of the unwanted in the life of a repentant soul. The power of darkness will be destroyed and be replaced by the power of the marvellous light of Christ. The spirit of lies will be cast away while the spirit of truth will take over. This transformation takes place during the purification of the body by water, blood and spirit which is called the immersion baptism.

1 JOHN 5:8

AND THERE ARE THREE THAT BEAR WITNESS ON EARTH, THE SPIRIT, THE WATER, AND THE BLOOD; AND THIS THREE AGREE AS ONE

It is also a stage of empowerment where the Holy Spirit will put a seal of redemption which is an anointing of power and glory. To this extent, the spirit is quickened and the battery charged for a great commission of the burden of the cross. Here the flesh is put under control while the spirit takes pre-eminence.

JOHN 6:63

IT IS THE SPIRIT WHO GIVES LIFE; THE FLESH PROFITS NOTHING. THE WORDS THAT I SPEAK TO YOU ARE SPIRIT, AND THEY ARE LIFE.

Eating The Body Of Christ And Drinking Of His Blood

JOHN 6:53-54

THEN JESUS SAID TO THEM, "MOST ASSUREDLY I SAY TO YOU, UNLESS YOU EAT THE FLESH OF THE SON OF MAN AND DRINK HIS BLOOD, YOU HAVE NO LIFE IN YOU. WHOEVER EATS MY FLESH AND DRINKS MY BLOOD HAS ETERNAL LIFE, AND I WILL RAISE HIM UP AT THE LAST DAY.

This is the second stage of transformation in the body of Christ; its necessity is to be united in one body and blood with Christ. This transition majorly forms the unique attributes of Christ in us, which originate from the blood of Jesus Christ. When we eat and drink in Holy Communion of the body and blood of our lord, there's always a mystery that manifest virtues of Christ in us. The virtue of patience, longsuffering, peace and charity. His blood is an empowerment to yield a strong faith and power of humility to carry our cross even to the death on the cross. His blood is life and while it flows in our vein it quicken us alive forever. While his body and blood forms a part of our life it becomes a covenant of strong hold that can never be broken. In this process in him we are complete.

COLLOSIANS 2:9-10

FOR IN HIM DWELLS ALL THE GODHEAD BODILY; AND YOU ARE COMPLETE IN HIM, WHO IS THE HEAD OF ALL PRINCIPALITIES AND POWER.

The Burden Of The Cross

MARK 8:34-38

WHEN HE HAD CALLED THE PEOPLE TO HIMSELF, WITH HIS DISCIPLES ALSO, HE SAID TO THEM, "WHOEVER DESIRES TO COME AFTER ME LET HIM DENY HIMSELF, AND TAKE UP HIS CROSS, AND FOLLOW ME.

FOR WHOEVER DESIRES TO SAVE HIS LIFE WILL LOSE IT, BUT WHOEVER LOSES HIS LIFE FOR MY SAKE AND THE GOSPEL'S WILL SAVE IT.

"FOR WHAT WILL IT PROFIT A MAN, IF HE GAINS THE WHOLE WORLD, AND LOSES HIS OWN SOUL?

"OR WHAT WILL A MAN GIVES IN EXCHANGE FOR HIS SOUL?

The burden of the cross is an issue of life and death. It is a decision that follows the principles of wisdom. Wisdom is the principal thing. The importance of this stage is to have the mind of Christ in us and to be radical in our decision to gain eternal life. The kingdom of God suffereth violence and the violent take it by force. It is a stage of radical decision to gain life or lose it. With the body of Christ and his blood in us, this will yield the virtues of longsuffering and faith of no turning back. To this end, our decision to carry the cross of burden must defy the strong arm of tribulation. It is through the burden of tribulation that we must gain eternal life. Jesus said "destroy this body and in three days I will build it." HIS blood in our life becomes a reactive element to move us positively to do exploit in the glory of the Lord.

ACTS 14:22

STRENGTHENING THE SOULS OF THE DISCIPLES, EXHORTING THEM TO CONTINUE IN THE FAITH, AND SAYING, "WE MUST THROUGH MANY TRIBULATIONS ENTER THE KINGDOM OF GOD."

The Reward Of Crown

REVELATIONS 3:11-12

"BEHOLD, I AM COMING QUICKLY! HOLD FAST WHAT YOU HAVE, THAT NO ONE MAY TAKE YOUR CROWN.

HE WHO OVERCOMES, I WILL MAKE HIM A PILLAR IN THE TEMPLE OF MY GOD, AND HE SHALL GO OUT NO MORE. I WILL WRITE ON HIM THE NAME OF MY GOD AND THE NAME OF THE CITY OF MY GOD. AND I WLL WRITE ON HIM MY NEW NAME.

The word of God have warned that Christ is coming shortly and those that overcome shall receive the crown. If you endure carrying the cross to the end your reward is guaranteed. Those who are in mount Zion shall not be moved, to stand on the rock of Christ is to be steadfast in righteousness desiring and seeking to please God always. Stand tall and strong for the Lord and be an effectual minister in the area of your calling. Bear witness for Christ as an oracle of God without the fear of adversity. Surely Christ who promised will not fail to reward your obedience.

2 TIMOTHY 4:8

FINALLY, THERE IS LAID UP FOR ME THE CROWN OF RIGHTEOUSNESS, WHICH THE LORD, THE RIGHTEOUS JUDGE, WILL GIVE TO ME ON THAT DAY, AND NOT TO ME ONLY BUT ALSO TO ALL WHO HAVE LOVED HIS APPEARING.

THE SEED OF THE EVERLASTING GOSPEL

GALATIANS 3:16:

"NOW TO ABRAHAM AND HIS SEED WERE THE PROMISES MADE, HE SAITH NOT, AND TO SEEDS, AS OF MANY; BUT AS OF ONE, AND TO THY SEEDS, WHICH IS CHRIST."

The eternal gospel is a seed of expected end that must be sowed and the sowers of this seed are the children of God. The owner of the seed is our father in heaven Jehovah Elohim the God of heaven and the earth. The seed of the eternal gospel and of the expected end is Jesus Christ the son of God, whose name is the word of God. The seed is life and light unto men of the earth. This seed becomes necessary and compulsory to be sown because it must bring life and light everlasting into the soul of man. The field to sow the seed is the world and the soil by which it grows is the heart of men and the fruit of the seed is the soul. The seed must be planted into every soul because all soul belongs to God, and God does not want any to perish.

2 PETER 3:9:

"THE LORD IS NOT SLACK CONCERNING HIS PROMISE, AS SOME MEN COUNT SLACKNESS, BUT IS LONG SUFFERING TO US-WARD NOT WILLING THAT ANY SHOULD PERISH, BUT THAT ALL SHOULD COME TO REPENTANCE.

God has charged every child of God for this great commission to carry the seed of eternal gospel for public enlightenment. Advocating for Jesus radically as an oracle of God and the ambassador of the word, proclaiming the message that Jesus is the lord, and saviour of the world, the way, the truth and life just as apostle Paul sowed his life for the gospel of Christ.

ROMANS 1:16:

"FOR I AM NOT ASHAMED OF THE GOSPEL OF CHRIST, FOR IT IS THE POWER OF GOD UNTO SALVATION TO EVERY ONE THAT BELIEVETH TO JEW FIRST, AND ALSO TO THE GREEK.

It is a great wisdom to win souls, why because God has commanded that we should bear fruit much more that will abide. Those who do not bear fruit shall be cut of, because with God we should not be a branch that is unfruitful. God will cast away every fruitless soul just as Jesus did to the fig tree. If you abide in him he will nourish you with the power of the Holy Spirit, and you will bear more fruit that will abide.

JOHN 15:2:

"EVERY BRANCH IN ME THAT BEARETH NOT FRUIT, HE TAKETH AWAY, AND EVERY BRANCH THAT BEARETH FRUIT, HE PURGETH IT, THAT IT MAY BRING FORTH MORE FRUIT.

Verse 8:

"HEREIN IS MY FATHER GLORIFIED THAT YE BEAR MUCH FRUIT; SO SHALL YE BE MY DISCIPLES".

PROVERB 11:30:

"THE FRUIT OF THE RIGHTEOUS IS A TREE OF LIFE, AND HE THAT WINNETH SOUL IS WISE.

This precious specie of seed is the one you sow alive and when it dies, it will resurrect eternal life just as Jesus died and resurrected eternal life for all. This is the seed which you are giving to sow for evangelism to yield everlasting soul. Evangelism is the mission of the lord and it is the will of the lord to bring light unto men of the earth. The light of God shines onto salvation to them that believe in him. Children of God have you tried to witness for Jesus today? Do you know it is your duty to influence the world for Jesus? Do not let the light in you show a shadow of yourself alone, let it overshadow the nation, tongues and kindred, for that is what the lord demands from you. You could save somebody's soul with the word of God, try it today and the Holy Spirit will perfect you and make you fishers of men.

You should bear the light of Christ in deed and in work, so that the world will see and come out of darkness.

JAMES 5:20:

"LET HIM KNOW THAT HE WHICH CONVERTETH THE SINNER FROM THE ERRORS OF HIS WAY SHALL SAVE A SOUL FROM DEATH, AND SHALL HIDE A MULTITUDE OF SIN.

SEQUENCE OF HIS WORD

1 PETER 4:7

"BUT THE END OF ALL THINGS IS AT HAND, BE YE THEREFORE SOBER, AND WATCH UNTO PRAYER.

2 PETER 3:9-11:

"BUT THE DAY OF THE LORD WILL COME AS A THIEF IN THE NIGHT, IN THE WHICH THE HEAVENS SHALL PASS AWAY WITH A GREAT NOISE, AND THE ELEMENTS SHALL MELT WITH FERVENT HEAT, THE EARTH ALSO AND THE WORKS THAT ARE THEREIN SHALL BE BURNT UP. SEEING THEN THAT ALL THESE THINGS SHALL BE DISSOLVED, WHAT MANNER OF PERSONS OUGHT YE TO BE IN ALL HOLY CONVERSATION AND GODLINESS.

God has sent his word to the people of the earth that the world and fullness thereof shall come to judgment, and then there shall be end. His word does not go void, the earth shall pass away but the word of God must come to pass. It is the sequential beginning that consequently brings the end. Adam and Eve faulted the foundation of the world which provoked God's anger to curse the land and the people of the earth, to live a life of sorrow. Adam and Eve derailed from the will and plan of God for life, from everlasting life to everlasting destruction. The world is growing according to God's word and his signs. There is an occultic inscription on the destiny of the world by the man of perdition, the prince of the world Satan that the world will go after vain things, vanity and forsake their maker the almighty God. This magic influence is controlling the mind of people of the world today, and has blinded them from the truth of life and reality.

2 CORINTHIANS: 4:4

"IN WHOM THE god OF THE WORLD HATH BLINDED THE MINDS OF THEM WHICH BELIEVE NOT, LEST THE LIGHT OF THE GLORIOUS GOSPEL OF CHRIST, WHO IS THE IMAGE OF GOD, SHOULD SHINE UNTO THEM.

Jesus Christ came to destroy the works of Satan. His word to the world is that the sheep shall be separated from the goat, praise God. On that day, Jesus opened the book of life, physically, the spirit of God was upon him and he declared it open to men of the world the word of prophet Isaiah that he has come to deliver the captive, to set free those who are bond by the grave of hell. Since then he continued to set free those who believe, he has removed the nails that fastened the sure ways of the grave of hell and let the bond free.

ISAIAH 22:25

"IN THAT DAY SAITH THE LORD OF HOSTS SHALL THE NAILS THAT IS FASTENED IN THE SURE PLACES BE REMOVED, AND BE CUT OFF FOR THE LORD HATH SPOKEN IT.

The truth remains forever that God has given his son Jesus the authority to judge the just and the unjust. Those things that are shakeable shall be shaken and be removed but the unshakable shall remain.

HEBREW 12:26-27

"WHOSE VOICE THEN SHOOK THE EARTH BUT NOW HE HATH PROMISED, SAYING, YET ONCE MORE I SHAKE NOT THE EARTH ONLY BUT ALSO

HEAVEN.AND THIS WORD, YET ONCE MORE, SIGNIFIETH THE REMOVING OF THOSE THINGS THAT ARE SHAKEN, AS OF THINGS THAT ARE MADE, THAT THOSE THINGS WHICH CANNOT BE SHAKEN MAY REMAIN.

The word of God is growing in sequence as he sent it and the world is growing according to the age by which he planted it and sooner it will come to a full age of harvest. We are waiting for the blast of the trumpet from heaven, and then the man of perdition will be revealed. Believe it, it is what you sow that you will reap, you sow in flesh, you will reap in flesh, you sow in spirit, you will reap in spirit. The body does not benefit the kingdom of God but the spirit; flesh and blood cannot inherit the kingdom of God. Two musicians from America sang a song which today depicts a meaning to the end time. The first is Michael Jackson who said in his song, "Let's make the world a better place to live". The second is Jim Reeves who sang, "The world is not my home, I am just passing by" Obviously the first speak for the world and standard of man, the understanding of the flesh. While the second speak for the kingdom of God with divine wisdom. The world cannot be a better place to live but rather a place of sorrow because it is accursed according to GOD's word. The Jews require for a sign and the Greek seek for wisdom but this is the word of the owner of the harvest.

MATTHEW 24:3

"AND AS HE SAT UPON THE MOUNT OLIVE, THE DISCIPLES CAME UNTO HIM PRIVATELY, SAYING, TELL US WHEN THIS THINGS SHALL BE? AND WHAT SHALL BE THE SIGNS OF THY COMING, AND OF THE END OF THE WORLD. AND JESUS ANSWERED AND SAID UNTO THEM. TAKE HEED THAT NO MAN DECIEVE YOU.

Let us critically study the signs with the events of today as Jesus said and convincingly draw a conclusion of the end;

1. **FOR MANY SHALL COME IN MY NAME, SAYING, I AM CHRIST, AND SHALL DECIEVE MANY.**

It's evident in the occult mystery today, that many has declared themselves messiah of the world and the world believed them and worship them, e.g. the Gopal das of Egypt, Guru Maraji of Nigeria and many others in the world, with the ministry of delusion.

2. **AND YE SHALL HEAR OF WARS AND RUMORS OF WARS.**

We are witness today that there are wars and rumours of wars almost all ends of the world, in Africa, Asia, Middle East and other continents.

3. **FOR NATION SHALL RISE AGAINST NATIONS AND KINGDOM AGAINST KINGDOMS.**

The Palestinians rose against Israel, Iraq against Iran, America against Russia, Iraq against Kuwait, Babylon has fallen the world rose against it which is Iraq today.

4. **THERE SHALL BE FAMINES.**

There is global economic recession in all parts of the world. Economic growth is at stand still in the world today.

5. **THERE SHALL BE PESTILENCE.**

Diseases abound today in our world both for human being and animals. Uncommon diseases ranging from HIV, CANCER, ANIMAL-FLU AND CURRENTLY EBOLA VIRUS

6. **THERE SHALL BE EARTHQUAKE.**

Earthquake is a frequent occurrence in most part of the world today; mostly in the Asian continent even recently in Haiti and China.

7. THEY SHALL DELIVER YOU UP TO BE AFFLICTED AND SHALL KILL YOU.

The apostles of Christ were afflicted in many ways and some were killed, and today the world is against true Christianity. Christians are humiliated and suffer the same fate as Jesus. They are outcasts of the society, and enemy of the world. The society is an adversity of the true Christian. In the northern part of Nigeria my country, Christians are massacred in large number by the boko haram group and so it is in other parts of the non-Christian countries of the world.

8. AND THEN SHALL MANY BE OFFENDED, AND SHALL BETRAY ONE ANOTHER, AND SHALL HATE ONE ANOTHER.

The society today are aggressive and offensive against one another, the love of neighbour is not in the global. Ninety five percent are self-centered, and evil minded against one another. This is an evidence of day to day occurrence in the society; diabolism and witchcraft practices, human rituals abound to destroy the lives of God's created.

9. AND MANY FALSE PROPHETS SHALL RISE AND DECIEVE MANY.

It is clear evidence today that the world has been invaded, by the workers of iniquity in the name of the ministers of God. The wolf in sheep's clothing without conscience using the name of the lord to serve Satan, and as well deceive the society to serve the vain god. They are those who speak of the goodness of their belly.

10. AND BECAUSE INIQUITY SHALL ABOUND AND LOVE OF MANY SHALL WAX COLD.

It is the pleasure of the world to dwell in sin, the word of God said that they did not like to retain God in their knowledge, because of this God gave them over to reprobate, to do those things that are not convenient. Being filled with all unrighteousness today, the world practice abnormal things like; Prostitution, Homosexuality, Bisexuality, Lesbianism, Gay marriage, and even having the boldness to establish the church of Satan.

11. **AND THIS GOSPEL OF THE KINGDOM SHALL BE PREACHED, IN THE ENTIRE WORLD FOR A WITNESS UNTO ALL NATIONS, AND THEN SHALL THE END COME** *(MATTHEW 24:14).*

Taking analysis of the event of the sign given, evidence is clearly seen and witnessed, that all the signs has been accomplished, the only thing remaining is for the gospel to reach each soul in the world, which missionaries are today in labour to bring to pass. The end could be any moment; the appointed time is not given. Knowing that this is the predicament, of the world, how have you washed your garment, waiting for the lord's coming? Be ready now for there shall be no excuse. Don't be among them that is asking for another sign, for the lord said no other sign shall be given than that of Jonah, who tarried for three days in the belly of a fish but still accomplished his mission. So also the lord shall accomplish his mission, though he may tarry. But will you repent like the people of Nineveh, who had this message of Jonah and repented of their sins. It is wise to make your decision now to avoid, "had I known". The lord is warning the world and souls to repent and come to him. This is not the time for ego and pride, of nations, great nations, super power, nuclear armament, peace upon the world, economic revival but it is the hour to answer the call of our God, and put our souls to eternal rest. To know that the duty of a man is to honour God and pay reverence unto him.

ECCLESIASTICS 12:13

"LET US HEAR THE CONCLUSION OF THE WHOLE MATTER, FEAR GOD AND KEEP HIS COMMANDMENTS, FOR THIS IS THE WHOLE DUTY OF MAN, FOR GOD SHALL BRING EVERY WORK INTO JUDGEMENT, WITH EVERY SECRET THING, WHETHER IT BE GOOD OR WHETHER IT BE EVIL.

THE SEAT OF JUDGEMENT

DANIEL 7:22

UNTIL THE ANCIENT OF DAYS CAME, AND JUDGMENT WAS GIVEN TO THE SAINTS OF THE MOST HIGH, AND THE TIME CAME THAT THE SAINTS POSSESSED THE KINGDOM.

The judgement of God is irreversible. Our God is just and gives a right judgement. There is the seat of judgement and there are also the appointed judges of eternal judgement. No shadow of doubt the word of God made it clear that the just shall judge the unjust. The saints are the panel of judges in the eternal seat of judgement; they will judge the world and the angels. The hour shall come when the angels of God shall gather the harvest of the vineyard of God. The son of God shall sit on his throne of judgement with his beloved, the children of obedience. They shall separate the sheep from the goat, and the verdict of his judgement shall be pronounced to every soul that sin against God.

MATHEW 25:31-34

WHEN THE SON OF MAN COMES IN HIS GLORY, AND ALL THE HOLY ANGELS WITH HIM, THEN HE WILL SEAT ON THE THRONE OF HIS GLORY. ALL THE NATIONS WILL BE GATHERED BEFORE HIM, AND HE WILL SEPARATE THEM ONE FROM ANOTHER AS A SHEPHERD DIVIDES HIS SHEEP FROM THE GOATS. AND HE WILL SET THE SHEEP ON HIS RIGHT HAND, BUT THE GOATS ON THE

> *LEFT. THEN THE KING WILL SAY TO THOSE ON HIS RIGHT HAND, COME, YOU BLESSED OF MY FATHER, INHERIT THE KINGDOM PREPARED FOR YOU FROM THE FOUNDATION OF THE WORLD.*

Apparently, the seed that man sow shall he reap at the end of all things. Peradventure you sow to the devil you shall harvest the portion of the wicked, brim stone and fire. The wise that sows in the labour of Christ in patience shall possess the eternal kingdom of God of the living. Those that turn their battle to the strait gate shall the son of man give the strength to endure till the end of time. Those whose passion is to gain the whole world take the fast lane in the broad way where lost souls are gathered in heap. Rather, blessed are those who do not stumble in the law of the Lord, their feet shall be established on the rock of ages. But those that err in the instructions of the Word surely have made an agreement with death and this agreement shall not be disannulled until they are trodden down by the judgement of God. The wages of sin is death and the free gift of God is eternal life.

ISAIAH 28:17

> *JUDGMENT ALSO WILL I LAY TO THE LINE AND RIGHTEONESS TO THE PLUMET AND THE HAIL SHALL SWEEP AWAY THE REFUGE OF LIES, AND THE WATERS SHALL OVERFLOW THE HIDDING PLACE.*

To escape the wrath of God's judgement is to yield a repentant heart because a broken and contrite heart shall every mortal soul submit to the Almighty God. The obedient spirit shall be exalted then the spirit of righteousness shall take pre-eminence. The Word of God planted in our spirit is in turn expected to bring forth the fruit of a gentle soul. Abhor that which is evil and cleave to that which is good, then your expectation to receive a just judgement shall not be cut off whether the judgement seat of Christ or the white throne judgement.

RETRIBUTION OF DIVINE JUSTICE

MATHEW 23:23

WOE UNTO YOU, SCRIBES AND PHARISEES, HYPOCRITES! FOR YE PAY TITHE OF MINT AND ANISE AND CUMMIN AND HAVE OMITTED THE WEIGHTIER MATTERS OF THE LAW, JUDGEMENT, MERCY AND FAITH: THESE OUGHT YE TO HAVE DONE, AND NOT TO LEAVE THE OTHER UNDONE.

Justice is a weight in a balance, mercy is an issue of love from a divine heart, faithfulness is a steadfast selfless sacrifice to someone you love. These three subject matters Jesus has told us, they are the weightier matters of the law in judgement. For divine justice in a balance, the word of God said that we should not judge that we may not be judged, because judgement is the authority of God. But if you are in authority to judge, judge a righteous judgement, that your judgement will fall in line with the justice of God, always remember the judgement that please God, loose the bands of wickedness, undo the heavy burdens and let the oppressed go free, draw out thy soul to the hungry, satisfy the afflicted soul and bear no false witness against your neighbour, "That which you wish others to do unto you, do it unto them." In this matter divine justice will find its place, for what you sow you shall reap.

ZECHARIAH 7:9-10

THUS SPEAKETH THE LORD OF HOSTS, SAYING, EXECUTE TRUE JUDGMENT, AND SHEW MERCY

*AND COMPASSIONS EVERY MAN TO HIS BROTHER
AND OPPRESS NOT THE WIDOW NOR THE
FATHERLESS, THE STRANGER, NOR THE POOR
AND LET NONE OF YOU IMAGINE EVIL AGAINST
HIS BROTHER IN YOUR HEART.*

Our God is merciful and have told us to be merciful, so that mercy can find its way to our situation. For the seed which you sow shall bear its fruit. Mercy is a divine justice; if God can forgive our trespasses why must we not forgive our neighbour his wrong doings to us. Mercy is a word of comfort to a Christian offender and repentance is the penalty of the offender. This tells us we must follow the doctrine of our lord. He taught us how to forgive one another, even the incident of a woman the scribes and Pharisees said they caught in the act of adultery. Jesus did not condemn her but asked a question that convicted their conscience. He said, "He that is without sin among you, let him first cast a stone at her" but none could find himself innocent to cast a stone at her but dispersed.

This made it clear to us that we should not judge because when we judge we might also condemn ourselves. The Bible said, forgive one another his trespasses and be merciful to one another.

LUKE 6:36-37

*BE YE THEREFORE MERCIFUL, AS YOUR FATHER
ALSO IS MERCIFUL. JUDGE NOT AND YE SHALL
NOT BE JUDGED: CONDEMN NOT, AND YE SHALL
NOT BE CONDEMNED: FORGIVE, AND YE SHALL
BE FORGIVEN:*

JOHN 8:10-11

*WHEN JESUS HAD LIFTED UP HIMSELF, AND SAW
NONE BUT THE WOMAN, HE SAID UNTO HER,
WOMAN, WHERE ARE THOSE THINE ACCUSERS?
HAD NO MAN CONDEMNED THEE? SHE SAID,
NO MAN, LORD. AND JESUS SAID UNTO HER,*

NEITHER DO I CONDEMN THEE: GO, AND SIN NO MORE.

Faith is the only way to believe and trust God. Jesus Christ sampled this opinion when he faithfully obeyed his father's word, why he said "father, if thou be willing remove this cup from me, nevertheless not my will, but thine will be done". Christ believed in the foundation of faithfulness of the word of his father, why he categorically told the Jews "Destroy this temple, and in three days I will raise it up". He has told us the essence of faithfulness, to be faithful to God because God will also be faithful to our life. Our faithfulness to one another is obedience to the law of God.

1 TIMOTHY 6:2

AND THEY THAT HAVE BELIEVING MASTERS, LET THEM NOT DESPISE THEM, BECAUSE THEY ARE BRETHREN; BUT RATHER DO THEM SERVICE,BECAUSE THEY ARE FAITHFUL AND BELOVED,PARTAKERS OF THE BENEFIT.THESE THINGS TEACH AND EXHORT.

THE RIGHTEOUS BRANCH

ISAIAH 11:1

AND THERE SHALL COME FORTH A ROD OUT OF THE STEM OF JESSE, AND A BRANCH SHALL GROW OUT OF HIS ROOTS:

A righteous branch is a member of the vine and belongs to the vine. A branch is not alone but grafted to the vine, and it is a dependent of the vine. A branch has not life of its own but sustain itself from the vine. The vine is not alone but depends on the root, the husbandman. Jesus Christ is the vine, the children of God are the branches and God is the husbandman to Christ. The branch is responsible for bearing fruits, they are the beauty and the glory of the vine because they produce flower and fruits which is the pride of the vine. The vine commissions the branch for the gift of ministry and in turn the branch is expected to bear fruits of the saints. The vine is holy and expects the branch which takes its spiritual nourishment from it to be holy indeed. The branch does not bear fruit of its own but the kind of the vine.

FOR IF THE FIRSTFRUIT IS HOLY, THE LUMP IS ALSO HOLY: AND IF THE ROOT BE HOLY, SO ARE THE BRANCHES.

Christ bearing his root through David on earth becomes a branch because he has come to bear fruits. But when Christ has beared fruits he became the vine, his disciples the branches and God the husbandman, because while in heaven he supplies their spiritual strength and nourishment as the vine but here on earth he carried the duty of his ministry which is bearing the fruits of his father as a branch.

JEREMIAH 23:5-6

BEHOLD THE DAYS COME, SAITH THE LORD, I WILL RAISE UNTO DAVID A RIGHTEOUS BRANCH, AND A KING SHALL REIGN AND PROSPER, AND SHALL EXECUTE JUDGEMENT AND JUSTICE IN THE EARTH. IN HIS DAYS JUDAH SHALL BE SAVED, AND ISREAL SHALL DWELL SAFELY: AND THIS IS HIS NAME WHEREBY HE SHALL BE CALLED, THE LORD OUR RIGHTEOUSNESS.

A righteous branch is an oracle of God, an ambassador of Christ ministry according to God's gift. He is expected to labour for Christ and to offer sacrifices acceptable unto God. He is always a delegate, a representative of Christ as a priest, evangelist, prophet, teacher and other ministries ordained by the unction of anointing power from on high. The most important is that a branch must bear much fruits that will abide to the vine. The branch as a vessel of service in the vineyard of God is not empty but a vessel with overflowing anointing.

ZECHARIAH 4:12-14

AND I ANSWERED AGAIN, AND SAID UNTO HIM, WHAT BE THESE TWO OLIVE BRANCHES WHICH THROUGH THE TWO GOLDEN PIPES EMPTY THE GOLDEN OIL OUT OF THEMSELVES? AND HE ANSWERED ME AND SAID, KNOWEST THOU NOT WHAT THESE BE? AND I SAID, NO, MY LORD.

THEN HE SAID THESE ARE THE TWO ANOINTED ONES THAT STAND BY THE LORD OF THE WHOLE EARTH.

AARON'S ROD BUDDED

NUMBERS 17:7-8

AND MOSES LAID UP THE RODS BEFORE THE LORD IN THE TABERNACLE OF WITNESS. AND IT CAME TO PASS, THAT ON THE MORROW MOSES WENT INTO THE TABERNACLE OF WITNESS; AND, BEHOLD, THE ROD OF AARON FOR THE HOUSE OF LEVI WAS BUDDED, AND BROUGHT FORTH BUDS, AND BLOOMED BLOSSOMS, AND YIELDED ALMONDS.

A priest is a Levite, chosen and divinely anointed as a minister of the altar of God. Because holiness is the sanctuary of God, he is anointed and consecrated to lift up offering and sacrifices to the holy God. Because he is close to God in holiness he becomes the favourite of God and has divine immunity. His chosen is a divine arrangement of the heavenly order because his calling and anointing is programmed for a purpose and plan of God. The ordination of the anointed priest of God is endorsed by the finger of God and by so doing his feet is on the rock of ages which makes it difficult for him to stumble at the push of the enemy. God fight his battles and rebuke the enemy on his behalf.

ZECHARIAH 3:2

AND THE LORD SAID UNTO SATAN, THE LORD REBUKE THEE, O SATAN; EVEN THE LORD THAT HAS CHOSEN JERUSALEM REBUKE THEE: IS NOT THIS A BRANCH PLUCK OUT OF FIRE?

Aaron could not stumble at the challenge of the enemy because his ministry was by divine arrangement of the almighty God. His rod budded and blossomed with almonds because he was the sceptre chosen as a first ordained priest of the most high God. God said no weapon fashioned against his anointed shall prosper because his righteousness is of God. Miriam contended with Moses but failed because he was chosen by God as an ordained deliverer who was faithful to God.

PSALM 105:14-15

HE SUFFERED NO MAN TO DO THEM WRONG: YEA, HE REPROVED KINGS FOR HIS SAKE SAYING, TOUCH NOT MY ANOINTED, AND DO MY PROPHET NO HARM.

God's anointing is a stronghold that cannot be broken easily. The anointing of David supersedes that of Saul because Saul was chosen in-between murmuring and complains of the children of Israel which did not follow supernatural laws and divine arrangement of the heavenly order. David as a chosen was a seal of anointing according to heavenly order, purpose and plan which was a manifest of God's prophesy to send his son to the earth through the root of Jesse and the throne of David. Saul committed sin and was rejected while David sinned against God and man but obtained mercy of God because of the covenant of God with him. This is the reason why the rod of his throne budded and blossomed with flowers while Saul's rod withered and the flowers faded.

PSALM 89:34-37

MY COVENANT WILL I NOT BREAK, NOR ALTER THE THING THAT IS GONE OUT OF MY LIPS. ONCE HAVE I SWORN BY MY HOLINESS THAT I WILL NOT LIE UNTO DAVID. HIS SEED SHALL ENDURE FOR EVER, AND HIS THRONE AS THE SUN BEFORE ME. IT SHALL BE ESTABLISHED FOR EVER AS THE MOON, AND AS A FAITHFUL WITNESS IN HEAVEN.

THE GOLDEN MANSION

JOHN 14:1-3

"LET NOT YOUR HEART BE TROUBLED, YOU BELIEVE IN GOD, BELIEVE ALSO IN ME. IN MY FATHERS HOUSE ARE MANY MANSIONS, IF IT WERE NOT SO, I WOULD HAVE TOLD YOU. I GO TO PREPARE A PLACE FOR YOU. AND IF I GO AND PREPARE A PLACE FOR YOU, I WILL COME AGAIN AND RECEIVE YOU TO MYSELF, THAT WHERE I AM, THERE YOU MAY BE.

Inheritance is of the lord and our possession is in the land of the living. Therefore seek ye the lord while you are on earth and do his will on earth as it is in heaven. Brethren, in patience continue in well doing, desire, and strive, seeking for glory, honour, peace, immortality and eternal life in the kingdom of the living. With heart full of conscience serve the God of eternity, lift up his name that is above all names, praise him that is worthy of praises, reverence him in his awesome presence. As a child of God walking in the path of righteousness, count yourself worthy of your father's legacy of inheritance.

LUKE 12:32

"FEAR NOT, LITTLE FLOCKS, FOR IT IS YOUR FATHER'S GOOD PLEASURE TO GIVE YOU THE KINGDOM.

If our hearts condemn us not we have confidence towards God and whatever we ask, we shall receive. But beware not to ask amiss in your lustful desire just as James and John demanded to seat at our father's right and left hand side and it was accounted to them as covetousness. Some seek to inherit the kingdom above while some have the opinion that earth is our place of inheritance. Whether the New Jerusalem on earth or heaven above the Lord reigneth, our portion is in the golden mansion of our Lord.

To fulfil all righteousness perform your spiritual obligations. If you love Jesus obey his commandment, be faithful and dedicated to our father's work. Be in pursuit of the course of holiness and perfection. Seek you the kingdom of God and its glory in earnest of heart, and your father who diligently rewards those that seek him in truth and in spirit will surely fulfil his divine promise to the children of obedience.

EPHESIANS 1:11

IN HIM ALSO WE HAVE OBTAINED AN INHERITANCE, BEING PREDESTINED ACCORDING TO THE PURPOSE OF HIM WHO WORKS ALL THINGS ACCORDING TO THE COUNSEL OF HIS WILL.

THE HOUSE UPON THE ROCK

PROVERB 15:24

*THE WAY OF LIFE IS ABOVE TO THE WISE THAT
HE MAY DEPART FROM HELL BENEATH"*

The house upon the rock is the house built through the knowledge and wisdom of God, its foundation is embedded on the rock of ages which never fail or collapse. There are two houses to build around our life. The one on the rock and the one on a sinking sand. The one on the rock is a foundation laid by Jesus Christ, and he is the pillar that holds the house. This house is the house of ascension which at the latter will ascend in glory to heaven. While the one on a sinking sand is the devils foundation, which is usually run by overflowing tide. Its nature is to descend into bottomless pit which is the devils domain. The unwise who build their house on sinking sand are after the world and vanity and by so doing, they gave out their soul to gain the whole world and become perpetually blind to the glory of eternity. The wise surrender their life unto Christ to build a home of everlasting life.

MATTHEW 7:24-27

*"THEREFORE WHOEVER LOVETH THIS SAYINGS
OF MINE, AND DOETH THEM, I WILL LIKEN HIM
UNTO A WISE MAN, WHICH BUILT HIS HOUSE
UPON A ROCK.*

*AND THE RAIN DESCENDED, AND THE FLOOD
CAME, AND THE WIND BLEW AND BEAT UPON*

THAT HOUSE, AND IT FELL NOT FOR IT WAS FOUNDED UPON A ROCK.

AND EVERY ONE THAT HEARETH THIS SAYING OF MINE, AND DOETH THEM NOT, SHALL BE LIKENED UNTO A FOOLISH MAN, WHO BUILT HIS HOUSE UPON THE SANDS.

AND THE RAIN DESCENDED, AND THE FLOOD CAME, AND THE WIND BLEW, AND BEAT UPON THE HOUSE, AND IT FELL, AND GREAT WAS THE FALL OF IT.

At the latter day, every shakeable shall be shaken and all unshakable shall remain. Every house or life built on the sand when the overflowing tide shall come; it shall be carried away to the lost Jesus Christ said, not even a stone on this building shall be left, everything shall be thrown down. Knowing what is good on time, a wise man should build his house not with the earthly materials but with the divine treasure of God.

MARK 13:1-2

"AND AS HE WENT OUT OF THE TEMPLE ONE OF HIS DISCIPLES SAITH UNTO HIM, MASTER, SEE WHAT MANNER OF STONES AND WHAT BUILDINGS ARE HERE.

AND JESUS ANSWERING SAID UNTO HIM, SEEST THOU THIS GREAT BUILDING? THERE SHALL NOT BE LEFT ONE STONE AGAINST ONE ANOTHER THAT SHALL NOT BE THROWN DOWN.

The great wisdom and knowledge of God is knowing the mystery of life and its treasures, which will help us to place life in its added value and preciousness. Then our decision to build a house of safety will clearly determine our love to our soul but carelessness to build a house of stubble, will spell a doom to our soul. The house of a man of wisdom is a house that ascends in glory to heaven while the house of unwise man is a house that will descend in shame to the pit. Abraham proved a great man of wisdom when he decided to walk with God rather than to follow the gods of his fathers. His wisdom brought glory to the house of Israel and light to the household of the gentiles. Noah proved having a great sense of knowledge of God when he obeyed God's instructions to preserve the souls of the believed Christians. He avoided the over running flood by his great wisdom.

PROVERB 1:6, 9

"WISDOM HATH BUILT HER HOUSE; SHE HATH HEWN OUT HER SEVEN PILLARS

FORSAKE THE FOOLISH, AND LIVE, AND GO IN THE WAY OF UNDERSTANDING. GIVE INSTRUCTION TO A WISE MAN, AND HE WILL BE YET WISER, TEACH A JUST MAN AND HE WILL INCREASE IN LEARNING.

REDEEMING THE TIME

EPHESIANS 5:15-17

"SEE THEN THAT YE WALK CIRCUMSPECTLY, NOT AS FOOL BUT AS WISE.

REDEEMING THE TIME, BECAUSE THE DAYS ARE EVIL.

WHEREFORE BE YE NOT UNWISE BUT UNDERSTANDING WHAT THE WILL OF THE LORD IS.

Man lives in the shadow of himself without understanding the inner circle of his life, the shrouded circumstances that surrounded the mystery of his life. The book of ecclesiastics 3:1 says, to everything there is a season and a time to every purpose under heaven. Time for good and time for bad, unpredictable circumstances and uncontrollable situations but to all these there is a determined and controlling power. This has been the fate of human kind that need to be redeemed with time to survive the things that are beyond him, this is the fate of good and bad. Man is supposed to be the architect of his own destiny, which he must achieve through divine wisdom. The total wisdom for a man with divine God is to submit his decision and action to God to surrender his life to the controlling power of all situations to overrule. The almighty God is the only one we can run to in a case of vagaries of situations. The word of God says, there is nothing too hard for him to do. Things we cannot change God will give us the grace to adapt. He is always there in time of trouble and in time of peace to make the situation a beautiful end.

PSALM 48:1-2

"GREAT IS THE LORD AND GREAT TO BE PRAISED IN THE CITY OF OUR GOD, IN THE MOUNTAIN OF HIS HOLINESS.

BEAUTIFUL FOR SITUATION, THE JOY OF THE WHOLE EARTH, IS MOUNT ZION ON THE SIDE OF THE NORTH, THE CITY OF THE GREAT KING.

We must learn to handle our predicaments and circumstances through God's wisdom by seeking the counselling of the word of God, to those things we have little understanding, and things we don't understand at all. Acknowledge God in all things that will permit perfection in our day to day life activities. Work with God in your situations and he will not fail to redeem your time for good. In your worst situations, do not seek for physical aid, but prayer and supplication, and request be made known unto God.

PHILIPPIANS 4:6

"BE CAREFUL FOR NOTHING BUT IN EVERYTHING BY PRAYER AND SUPPLICATION, WITH THANKSGIVING LET YOUR RESQUEST BE MADE KNOWN UNTO GOD.

If we look at the brevity of life from only a human perspective, life begins to look like a waste of time. Why build up an inheritance to leave to someone who will waist it? Why obtain a great name when no one will remember it? And why accomplish great works that will one day be forgotten? If this is all there is to life, then we will agree with the wise man Solomon who said he hate life.

ECCLESIASTICS 2:14

"THEREFORE I HATE LIFE, BECAUSE THE WORD THAT IS WROUGHT UNDER THE SUN IS

*GREVIOUS UNTO ME, FOR ALL IS VANITY AND
VEXATION OF SPIRIT.*

It is meaningless if we depend on the things of this life to find a sense of purpose and accomplishment. Life has a meaning and purpose, the real purpose of life is to serve God. It is during this life that we prepare for eternity and build up treasures in heaven and stop pursuing shadows.

Therefore let us nourish our faith in the infinite power of his mercy, the overseer of life who knows the days of prosperity and the days of adversity. He is there for those who believe in his son Jesus, he will not allow the over running flood to swallow his children.

ECCLESIASTICS 7:14

*"IN THE DAYS OF PROSPERITY, BE JOYFUL BUT
IN THE DAYS OF ADVERSITY, CONSIDER. GOD
ALSO HATH SENT THE ONE OVER AGAINST THE
OTHER, TO THE END THAT MEN SHOULD FIND
NOTHING AFTER HIM.*

THE GREAT PURPOSE OF LIFE

ECCLESIASTICS 12:13-14

"LET US HEAR THE CONCLUSION OF THE WHOLE MATTER, FEAR GOD AND KEEP HIS COMMANDMENT, FOR THIS IS THE WHOLE DUTY OF MAN.

FOR GOD SHALL BRING EVERY WORK INTO JUDGEMENT, WITH EVERY SECRET THING WHETHER IT BE GOOD OR WHETHER IT BE EVIL.

The will of God to create mankind is for man to serve him, reverence unto him, and be obedient to his words and to dwell in his presence at all time. Every individual, a soul that God created has a mission on earth and a call unto the lord. We are not just spectators in this event of call in the lord; we are a role model unto good work in the lord. We are vessels unto use not just empty containers, but vessels of purpose, expected to be effectual and full of service to the master. In the great house of God, we are not just bench warmers, or members of the house of God only, but servants of the lord in high esteem, we are here to give in our spiritual or physical strength to serve the lord without being weary or faint.

EXODUS 23:24-25

"THOU SHALL NOT BOW DOWN TO THY GODS, NOR SERVE THEM, NOR DO AFTER THEIR WORKS: BUT THOU SHALL UTTERLY OVER THROW THEM, AND QUITE BREAK DOWN THEIR IMAGES, AND

*YE SHALL SERVE THE LORD YOUR GOD, AND HE
SHALL BLESS THY BREAD, AND THY WATER, AND
I WILL TAKE SICKNESS AWAY FROM THE MIDST
OF THEE.*

If we have the zeal to serve our God, it should be in a greater height, for he is a rewarder of them that diligently seek him. For them that believe receive his power, and the spirit of God manifest in them diverse gifts, to empower them for greater work in the lord. This is not by might neither power, but by the spirit of the living God. If our desire is sincere, the Holy Spirit will manifest in us diverse gifts, to aid us for a perfect work in the house of God, and fulfil the purpose of God in our life.

In the house of God we work to be honoured and not to be dishonoured, we must work in sanctification according to the unction of the Holy Spirit for our God to glorify our work as to bring honour to his name. Not according to human endeavour but following the direction of the Holy Spirit, for a good finishing, of course, your crown awaits you.

2 TIMOTHY 2:20-21

*"BUT IN A GREAT HOUSE THERE ARE NOT ONLY
VESSELS OF GOLD AND OF SILVER, BUT ALSO OF
WOOD AND OF EARTH AND SOME TO HONOR,
AND SOME TO DISHONOR.*

*IF A MAN PURGES HIMSELF FROM THESE, HE
SHALL BE A VESSEL UNTO HONOR, SANCTIFIED
AND FIT FOR THE MASTER'S USE, AND UNTO
EVERY GOOD WORK.*

Our work on earth has an end; it might be a long term bases or short term bases, only the lord knows. John the Baptist came for a short term mission as well as Jesus came for a short term mission. Our work on earth for the lord does not need us to waste time, what we are to do we must do fast to meet up with the date line, to avoid half hazard work.

JOHN 9:4

"I MUST WORK THE WORKS OF HIM THAT SENT ME, WHILE IT IS DAY, THE NIGHT COMETH, WHEN NO MAN CAN WORK.

BE YE NOT SERVANT OF MAN BUT SERVANT OF THE LORD

1 CORINTHIANS 7:23

"YE ARE BOUGHT WITH A PRICE, BE NOT YE THE SERVANT OF MEN.

Our life is a call unto the lord. We are to fit in with the plans and purpose of the almighty God for our life, we are here to serve him and be a pleasure to him because he created us for his pleasure. The earth is the lord and fullness thereof, the lord owns us, he bought us with costly price, so we are in bond to serve him all the days of our life. We are necessary co-workers in the vineyard of the lord. And we have a yoke of agreement, to serve him but not like a slave, because he made his yoke easy, and not with heavy burden. Just as one who has left Egypt with joy to the promise land. Our service should not be with complains, murmuring or eye service, but rendering service as a sacrifice of sweet smelling saviour.

EPHESIANS 6:6-8

"NOT WITH EYE SERVICE, AS MEN PLEASERS, BUT AS THE SERVANT OF CHRIST, DOING THE WILL OF GOD FROM THE HEART.

WITH GOOD WILL, DOING SERVICE, AS TO THE LORD, AND NOT TO MEN. KNOWING THAT WHATSOEVER GOOD THING ANY MAN DOETH, THE SAME SHALL HE RECEIVE OF THE LORD, WHETHER HE BE BOND OR FREE.

Honour should be giving to whom that merit honour. The Lord Jesus Christ was bruised, mocked, humiliated, and he died on the Calvary, for our sake to purchase our soul for a costly price. He is the bishop of our soul. He deserves your honest commitment in service rather than your service to men of the world, our physical strength and spiritual strength should be utilized to honour the lord in service. Our life should be an offering unto the lord, whole and holy, a total duty to the lord's pleasure; it should not be a compromise to the desire of the world.

He was humiliated, despised, buffeted, but like a lamb about to be slaughtered, he faithfully carried our sorrows away, this is his precious service to man, to give man a place of glory. What is your good service to appreciate him in this manner of sacrifice? This was for your sake, to redeem you for glory.

Aaron disappointed God, he ran out of patience and faith, and decided to serve man instead of God who called him to serve. He obeyed man's demand and ignored God's instruction. He has forgotten that his call is to please his maker, but instead of serving God, he deviated to serve man and idol, thereby committing serious abomination to his God. Our God is a jealous God; he will never share his glory with another god. You cannot serve God and at the same time serve mammon. God is holy and cannot rub shoulders with unholy gods.

EXODUS 32:8-10

"THEY HAVE TURNED ASIDE QUICKLY OUT OF THE WAY WHICH I COMMANDED THEM THEY HAVE MADE THEMSELVES A MOLTEN CALF, AND HAVE WORSHIPPED IT, AND HAVE SACRIFICED THEREUNTO, AND SAID, THESE BE THY GOD O ISREAL, WHICH HAVE BROUGHT THEE UP OUT OF THE LAND OF EGYPT. AND THE LORD SAID UNTO MOSES, I HAVE SEEN THESE PEOPLE, AND BEHOLD, IT IS A STIFFNECKED PEOPLE.

NOW THEREFORE LET ME ALONE THAT MY WRATH MAY WAX HOT AGAINST THEM, AND I WILL MAKE OF THEE A GREAT NATION.

Josiah is a typical example of a man who served God contrary to what Aaron did. After his reading of the book of the covenant to the hearing of his people, he stood by the pillar and made a covenant before the lord to walk in his ways and to obey all his commandment and laws, with all his heart and with all his soul, to live up to the word of the covenant. He sanctified the house of the lord by banishing the idol worshippers and their priests, he served God in uprightness, and he pleased his God instead of pleasing the world and his people.

2 KINGS 23:1-3

"AND THE KING SENT, AND THEY GATHERED UNTO HIM, ALL THE ELDERS OF JUDAH AND JERUSALEM, AND THE KING WENT UP INTO THE HOUSE THE LORD, AND ALL THE MEN OF JUDAH, AND ALL THE INHABITANTS OF JERUSALEM, WITH HIM AND THE PRIEST AND PROPHETS, AND ALL THE PEOPLE BOTH SMALL AND GREAT AND HE READ IN THERE EARS ALL THE WORDS OF THE BOOK OF THE COVENANTS, WHICH WAS FOUND IN THE HOUSE OF THE LORD, AND THE KING STOOD BY A PILLAR, AND MADE A COVENANT BEFORE THE LORD TO WALK AFTER THE LORD, AND TO KEEP HIS COMMANDMENTS AND HIS TESTIMONIES, AND HIS STATUS WITH ALL THEIR HEARTS AND ALL THEIR SOUL TO PERFORM THE WORDS OF THIS COVENANT THAT WERE WRITTEN IN THIS BOOK, AND ALL THE PEOPLE STOOD TO THE COVENANT.

MAN SHALL NOT LIVE BY BREAD ALONE BUT BY EVERY WORD OF GOD

DEUTERONOMY 8:3

"AND HE HUMBLED THEE AND SUFFERED THEE, TO HUNGER AND FED THEE WITH MANNA, WHICH THOU KNOWEST NOT, NEITHER DID THY FATHER KNOW, THAT HE MIGHT MAKE THEE KNOW, THAT MAN DOTH NOT LIVE BY BREAD ONLY, BUT EVERY WORD THAT PROCEEDETH OUT OF THE MOUTH OF THE LORD, DOTH MAN LIVE.

Man came into the world believing in pleasures of the world, in the fulfilment of the desire of his flesh. That was the strong hold of Satan to lure man into sin to lose his dominion. The earthy body of man was a great distraction to his life that he lost focus to God's instructions to his well being. Man's idea of life is to satisfy the body, by so doing subjected his spirit to obey the laws of the flesh. He becomes more or less a living soul, without a perfect functioning spirit, which becomes detrimental to the soul of the kingdom.

JOHN 6:63

"IT IS THE SPIRIT THAT QUICKENETH, THE FLESH PROFITHETH NOTHING, THE WORDS

THAT I SPEAK UNTO YOU, THEY ARE SPIRIT AND THEY ARE LIFE.

The last Adam which is Christ came with the quickening spirit to give life to our mortal body for us to receive the power of the spirit that we may not continue to depend on the flesh which is foreign in the kingdom of our hope. The spirit is of eternal and will inherit eternal life. Jesus Christ is the immortal word of God that proceeded out of God's mouth, if we receive him; we have received the power to overcome the world and the flesh. Jesus obeyed the word of God, and the spirit of God came upon him on the day of his baptism, he became of the spirit rather than flesh of the dead. By the anointing of the Holy Spirit upon his life, he was empowered to overcome Satan's temptation in the wilderness. Even as the devil used flesh as a weak point to destroy the purpose of God in his life, by asking him to eat bread in the days of his forty days and forty nights fasting and praying. But the spirit in him quickened him of his father's word, and in the manner of the sword of the spirit, he reminded Satan of God's word that says. "Man shall not live by bread alone but by every word that proceed out of God's mouth". Jesus Christ became a living example for us to live a victorious life in this circumstance. By applying this strategy, we will overcome all avenues of devil's temptations, by obeying the word of God and disobeying the demand of the flesh.

By the word of God, we were created, by his word we were destroyed, because of obeying the call of flesh, and by his mercy, he quickened us by his word. His word is a compass to our life, and we cannot do without his word, because it is the truth, and the way to life. For us to inherit the kingdom, we must not live by eating or drinking, satisfying the flesh as Adam and Eve became a victim, but obeying the will of God for our life is wisdom. If anyone wants to eat and drink, let him eat and drink, in the manner of sanctification of the spirit. Not eating the bread of decay, but the bread of life, which is the word of God? Jesus is the word of God, the word to obey and live.

JOHN 6:51

"I AM THE LIVING BREAD, WHICH CAME DOWN FROM HEAVEN, IF ANY MAN EAT OF THIS BREAD,

*HE SHALL LIVE FOR EVER, AND THE BREAD THAT
I WILL GIVE IS MY FLESH, WHICH I WILL GIVE
FOR THE LIFE OF THE WORLD.*

Daniel was moved by the spirit that he adhered to God's instructions not to defy himself with the food of the mammons in the palace of the Babylonian king. Joseph acted in the spirit when he refused to be lured into sin by Potipher's wife. That was a gate way to his victorious life, and should be an example for a victorious Christian life.

1 PETER 4:1-3

*"FOR AS MUCH THEN AS CHRIST HAS SUFFERED
FOR US IN THE FLESH, ARM YOURSELVES
LIKEWISE WITH THE SAME MIND, FOR HE THAT
HAS SUFFERED IN THE FLESH, HAS CEASED
FROM SIN.*

*THAT HE NO LONGER SHOULD LIVE THE REST
OF HIS TIME IN THE FLESH, TO THE LUST OF
MEN, BUT TO THE WILL OF GOD.*

*FOR THE TIME PAST OF OUR LIFE MAY SUFFICE US
TO HAVE WROUGHT THE WILL OF THE GENTILES,
WHEN WE WALK IN LASCIVIOUSNESS, LUSTS,
EXCESS OF WINE, REVELLINGS, BANQUETING,
AND ABOMINABLE IDOLATRIES.*

LOOKING UNTO THE CROSS

1 CORINTHIANS 11:24-26

AND WHEN HE HAD GIVEN THANKS, HE BROKE IT, AND SAID, TAKE EAT, THIS IS MY BODY, WHICH IS BROKEN FOR YOU, TAKE THIS IN REMEMBRANCE OF ME.

AFTER THE SAME MANNER ALSO HE TOOK THE CUP, WHEN HE HAD SUPPED, SAYING THIS CUP IS THE NEW TESTAMENT IN MY BLOOD, THIS DO AS OFT AS YE DRINK IT IN REMEMBRANCE OF ME.

FOR AS OFTEN AS YE EAT THIS BREAD AND DRINK THIS CUP, YE DO SHOW LORD'S DEATH TILL HE COMES.

When we take our mind to memory lane of the death and rise of the glorious ascension of our lord Jesus Christ, what do we imagine? And what impression do you create in your mind? For a worldly fellow who dwell in the flesh, and sing praises of the world's standard, will see the place of Calvary as an abandoned place called Golgotha, the place of skull. This is where criminals are executed, and it becomes a place also our lord was crucified. To the worldly man he is justified to celebrate our lord's freedom to life with artificial emotion, and mockery of commitment. Having an ulterior motive, he will clinch to practicing religion rather than Christianity as the case may be. Serving the almighty God in the outer mind, and loving the world in the inner mind, thereby creating enmity with the God of righteousness. But to the good conscience, the committed

Christians who understand the essence of the Calvary will celebrate the death of Christ on the Calvary as a freedom of Passover, from the land of the dead to the land of the living, from Egypt to promise land through the wilderness. Ultimately, his death on the Calvary becomes a shadow of our commitment spiritually to achieve the eternal life.

Eating and drinking in the same cup Jesus drank as children of God makes it imperative, that we must carry our cross and follow him, and share in the burden of his temptations. It is in this bid that He wants us to reclaim our lost life, through his examples which he has laid as a foundation with his blood on the Cross of Calvary.

1 PETER 2:21

"FOR EVEN HERE UNTO WHERE YE CALLED, BECAUSE CHRIST ALSO SUFFFERED FOR US AN EXAMPLE, THAT YE SHOULD FOLLOW HIS STEPS.

He told us not to lose focus, but keep in the faith, determined and walk separated from every manner of evil. In faith and patience our life should challenge the tribulations of this world as the devil will project them along our way in this kingdom journey. We should be aggressive in facing temptations and persecution of the world, as Jesus did reprimand the world that he cannot be stopped from accomplishing his father's work, here on earth. While he said,

JOHN 2:19

"JESUS ANSWERED AND SAID UNTO THEM, DESTROY THIS TEMPLE AND IN THREE DAYS I WILL RAISE IT.

MATTHEW 16:21-24

"THEN PETER TOOK HIM AND BEGAN TO REBUKE HIM SAYING, 'BE IT FAR FROM THE LORD, THIS SHALL NOT BE UNTO THEE'

BUT HE TURNED AND SAID UNTO PETER, GET THEE BEHIND ME SATAN, THOU ART AN OFFENCE UNTO ME, FOR THOU SAVOURETH NOT THE THINGS THAT BE OF GOD, BUT THOSE THAT BE OF MEN, THEN SAID JESUS UNTO HIS DISCIPLES, IF ANY MAN WILL COME AFTER ME, LET HIM DENY HIMSELF AND TAKE HIS CROSS AND FOLLOW ME.

Our lord Jesus came into the world with a triumphant entry. The entrance of his birth gave way to our adoption into the family of God, the entrance of his death destroyed our earthly body on the cavalry, which is insignificant in the kingdom of God, then the entrance of his risen, resurrected our soul into heavenly glory. Then whose sons or daughters are you? The one that draw back into perdition? Or believe in the saving of soul? There is no replacement to the soul that sin, and every soul that sin shall die. Loose not focus but understand the necessities of the body of Christ on the cavalry.

ONE THING THOU LACKEST

2 CORINTHIANS 4:3-5

"BUT IF OUR GOSPEL BE HID, IT IS HEED TO THEM THAT ARE LOST.

IN WHOM THE GOD OF THIS WORLD HATH BLINDED THE MINDS OF THEM WHICH BELIEVE NOT, LEST THE LIGHT OF THE GLORIOUS GOSPEL OF CHRIST, WHO IS THE IMAGE OF GOD, SHOULD SHINE UNTO THEM.

The perverse generation of this day, take delight in the glory of the earth than they take pleasure in the things of God. They believe in religious Christianity rather than salvation Christianity. They want to reach to God without any invitation or without any laws or rules check-mating them. Their Joy is to serve God with carefree attitude, in their own self righteous interest. The world claim to know the almighty God, the God whom they denied publicly and refuse to honour and glorify. The orthodox churches missed the facts in the sacred doctrine of Christianity and misinterpreted it to be the form of religion and spiritualism. If their glory is good, why is there division in the church? If the Holy Spirit is not revealing their hidden agenda, why the confusion and misunderstanding, in their doctrine setting. Why some supporting the power of the Holy Spirit and some are condemning it. Our God is not author of confusion. If there is no issue in catholic today, why is the charismatic movement an offence to the church? If there is no issue in Anglican why is EFAC an offence to the church? If all is well in the Moslem setting why the often crises and shedding of blood among themselves, being hindrance to the peace of humanity. They call it an injunction rather than doctrine. If the white garment churches have no issue with the born again, why not keep straight the doctrine of Christianity instead of practicing Christianity as a place of power arena thereby missing the whole purpose of Christianity which is salvation.

1 CORINTHIANS 5:6-7

"YOUR GLORY IS NOT GOOD, KNOW YOU NOT THAT A LITTLE LEAVEN LEAVENETH THE WHOLE LUMP. PURGE OUT THEREFORE THE OLD LEAVEN THAT YE MAY BE A NEW LUMP, AS YE ARE UNLEAVENED, FOR EVEN CHRIST OUR PASSOVER IS SACRIFICED FOR US.

The book of 2 Timothy revealed their inner self, and what they portrayed outside themselves.

2 TIMOTHY 3:4-7

"TRAITORS, HEADY, HIGH-MINDED, LOVERS OF PLEASURES, MORE THAN LOVERS OF GOD, HAVING A FORM OF GODLINESS, BUT, DENYING THE POWER THEREOF, FROM SUCH TURN AWAY,

FOR OF THIS SOUGHT ARE THEY WHICH CREEP INTO HOUSES AND LEAD CAPTIVES SILLY WOMEN LADEN WITH SINS, LAID AWAY WITH DIVERS LUSTS.

EVER LEARNING, AND NEVER ABLE TO COME TO THE KNOWLEDGE OF THE TRUTH.

Now it is quite understandable that there is something amiss in the circle of these acclaimed believers of Christ, something lacking in their life style that need to be fixed, to bring perfection in their Christian life. That thing lacking is the perfect master Jesus Christ of Nazareth. All religious setting need Jesus Christ, churches of flesh need Jesus Christ, the society Christianity need Jesus Christ, you can serve Jesus Christ if you change your attitude and approach towards serving God. This is what exactly the two rulers of the Jews, the religious leaders did in other to have understanding on how to inherit the kingdom of God.

LUKE 18:22

NOW WHEN JESUS HEARD THESE THINGS HE SAID UNTO HIM, YET LACKEST THOU ONE THING, SELL ALL THY HAST, AND DISTRIBUTE UNTO THE POOR, AND THOU SHALL HAVE TREASURE UNTO HEAVEN, AND COME FOLLOW ME.

God is spirit and cannot be worshipped in flesh. The true worship of God comes from the spirit, the spirit of God and your spirit bearing witness that you are a child of God. God has given us the spirit of the lord that we might worship him to his expectation and perfection.

GALATIANS 4:6

"AND BECAUSE YE ARE GOD'S SONS, GOD HATH SENT FORTH THE SPIRIT OF HIS SON INTO YOUR HEARTS, CRYING ABBA FATHER.

The spirit is righteous but the flesh is unrighteous. God is spirit and he is righteous, we must follow the ways of the lord, he is spirit and his righteousness is in the spirit. We must follow the ways of the spirit of God to achieve perfection in serving the God of heaven.

THE KINGDOM OF GOD COMETH NOT WITH OBSERVATION

REVELATION 21:3

"AND I HEARD A GREAT VOICE OUT OF HEAVEN SAYING, BEHOLD, THE TABERNACLE OF GOD IS WITH MEN, AND HE WILL DWELL WITH THEM, AND THEY SHALL BE HIS PEOPLE, AND GOD HIMSELF SHALL BE WITH THEM AND BE THEIR GOD.

The kingdom of God is here on earth to them that believe in the son of God, they shall receive the promise. The kingdom of God does not come by watching from the outside, or by observation, not by ceremony or expectation, neither by general experience nor by public event. It comes by personal experience, a divine encounter with God. The kingdom of God is not outside but within us. It is all about God's intervention in our personal life that establishes the kingdom in our individual life. The kingdom of God is a decision by a willing heart, the heart that has received the divine God. If you open the door of your heart to the owner of the kingdom, he shall come in and establish with you.

LUKE 17:20-21,

"AND WHEN HE WAS DEMANDED OF THE PHARISEES WHEN THE KINGDOM OF GOD

SHOULD COME, HE ANSWERED AND SAID, THE KINGDOM OF GOD COMETH NOT WITH OBSERVATION

NEITHER SHALL THEY SAY, LO HERE OR LO THERE FOR BEHOLD, THE KINGDOM OF GOD IS WITHIN YOU.

Jesus Christ is the tabernacle of God, who has come to dwell in the midst of his people. Unto Him the lord of host shall people gather in fellowship to serve their God. To them that genuinely receive him and believe in him, he shall give the power of the holy ghost to serve in his father's vineyard. The kingdom of God is a great open door to possess, but the world and the prince of the world are against it. So the decision to possess the kingdom must come from a gigantic heart, the hearts that can never be influenced by the world. To possess the gate of heaven you need force and violence to silence the power of adversaries.

MATTHEW 11:12

"AND FOR THE DAYS OF JOHN THE BAPTIST UNTIL NOW, THE KINGDOM OF GOD SUFFERETH VIOLENCE, AND THE VIOLENCE TAKE IT BY FORCE.

To reach the kingdom is to accept Jesus Christ as your personal saviour and lord. And the process to achieve the kingdom of God is to follow Jesus Christ to tread through the wilderness of trials and temptations, just as the Israelites tread through the wilderness to the promise land. Remember in this journey, you are not alone, the Holy Spirit is your company and ready to lead you home if you abide in the holiness of God. He who promise is faithful and will accomplish his promise as He did fulfil his promise to Abraham, Isaac and Jacob, even to David and Solomon.

DANIEL 7:18

"BUT THE SAINTS OF THE MOST HIGH SHALL TAKE THE KINGDOM, AND POSSESS THE KINGOM FOR EVER, EVEN FOR EVER AND EVER.

Procrastination to the kingdom of God is the devil's weapon. The power of repentance comes from the God of light; determination is a perfect step to climb the ladder that goes to heaven.

TAKE MY YOKE UPON YOU

1 TIMOTHY 6:2-3

"LET AS MANY SERVANTS AS ARE UNDER THE YOKE COUNT THEIR OWN MASTER WORTHY OF HONOR THAT THE NAME OF GOD AND DOCTRINE IS NOT BLASPHAMED.

AND THEY THAT HAVE BELIEVING MASTERS, LET THEM NOT DESPISE THEM BECAUSE THEY ARE BRETHREN, BUT RATHER DO THEM SERVICE, BECAUSE THEY ARE FAITHFUL AND BELOVED, PARTAKERS OF THE BENEFIT. THESE THINGS TEACH AND EXORT.

The saviour of the world who came to take the burden of our life took our cares upon him and made an invitation to the troubled world, the world that travail with hopelessness. His invitations was to the men of the world, inviting all that labour and are heavy laden, to come unto him and have their rest from the troubled world. It was a word of comfort and assurance to the world for a new hope, for them who are willing to give up with the hopeless life and follow Jesus for an eternal rest in their life. Our lord wants all souls to respond to this call and at the same time denounce the yoke of sin, and take the yoke of righteousness which is a bond to abide in the lord for effectual service and promise of eternal life.

MATTHEW 11:28-30

"COME UNTO ME ALL YE THAT LABOR AND ARE HEAVY LADEN, AND I WILL GIVE YOU REST.

TAKE MY YOKE UPON YOU AND LEARN OF ME, FOR I AM MEEK AND LOWLY IN HEART, AND YE SHALL FIND REST UNTO YOUR SOULS.

FOR MY YOKE IS EASY AND MY BURDEN IS LIGHT.

The yoke of Jesus Christ is the yoke of fellowship unto God. It is an accord between you and the lord to render a selfless service with a holy heart, with the seal of the Holy Spirit in a common willingness to obey God. To whom ye yield yourself a servant to obey, his servant ye are. Now you are a servant of the righteous, it becomes essential that you are a necessary co-worker in the vineyard of God of righteousness. In every day of your life, you shall abide in the yoke by which you are sealed. Fellowship with Christ day by day which is a good service, serve him with all your strength, power and might to bear good fruit in him.

ROMANS 6:16

"KNOW YE NOT THAT TO WHOM YE YEILD YOURSELF SERVANTS TO OBEY, HIS SERVANTS YE ARE, WHETHER OF SIN UNTO DEATH OR OF OBEDIENCE UNTO RIGHTEOUSNESS.

Jesus Christ is the vine in the vineyard of God, the shepherd in the house of God. If we have taken the yoke of Jesus Christ which is easy and his burden which is light, we must abide in him. We must not live in isolation because we must learn from him the ways of meek and lowly heart. We are the branch which must abide to the vine, so we could have his nature of humility and obedience which is our yoke in righteousness.

PHILIPPIANS 2:7-8

"BUT MADE HIMSELF OF NO REPUTATION, AND TOOK UPON HIM THE FORM OF A SERVANT, AND WAS MADE IN THE LIKENESS OF MAN,

> *AND BEING FOUND IN FASHION AS A MAN, HE HUMBLED HIMSELF AND BECAME OBEDIENT UNTO DEATH EVENS THE DEATH OF THE CROSS.*

This is our cross, to follow Jesus Christ and obey his words in deed and in action.

THE BURDEN OF THE CROSS BEFORE THE CROWN OF THE THRONE

1 PETER 4:12-14

"BELOVED, THINK IT NOT STRANGE CONCERNING THE FIERY TRIAL WHICH IS TO TRY YOU, AS THOUGH SOME STRANGE THING HAPPENED UNTO YOU.

BUT REJOICE IN AS MUCH AS YE ARE PARTAKERS OF CHRIST'S SUFFERINGS, THAT WHEN HIS GLORY SHALL BE REVEALED, YE MAY BE GLAD ALSO WITH EXCEEDING JOY.

IF YE BE REPROACH FOR THE NAME OF CHRIST, HAPPY ARE YE, FOR THE SPIRIT OF GLORY AND GOD GRACE RESTETH UPON YOU. ON THIER PART HE IS EVIL SPOKEN OF, BUT ON YOUR PATH HE IS GLORIFIED.

The reality of a child of God in the road to the strait gate is a necessary long suffering. The road is narrow, and a path to the cross, so the burden of the cross is upon the shoulder, and its content is of trials and temptations. As a soldier of hardness as Paul said we should be, you are expected to bear a true witness of Christ as an oracle of God, without fear of man or evil. Your banner is faith and courage with patience, persevering the long suffering but bearing in mind that one with Christ is not alone, the spirit of the living God is your comforter. He knows the road is lonely and narrow, he will not leave you on your own, and He will come to lead you home, if you genuinely carry your cross without fear of the adversity.

JAMES 1:12

"BLESSED IS THE MAN THAT ENDURETH TEMPTATION, FOR WHEN HE IS TRIED, HE SHALL RECEIVE THE CROWN OF LIFE, WHICH THE LORD HAS PROMISED TO THEM THAT LOVE HIM,

Every child of God has a challenge to carry his cross just as the lord commanded Paul to carry his cross and suffer all manner of things for him. Along the way is the field of serpent which keep in wait to bruise our feet, while we also have the authority to bruise their head as the divine law stipulate. So it is not a journey of merry go round or fanfare, but a battle front to lose the crown or to possess it for everlasting. If you are a child of God or man of God, and devil did not challenge the divine power in you or your anointing, then it is necessary for you to review your anointing, if it is of the lord or if it is an anointing of error. As long as you bear the truth and light of God, the gods of the darkness will war against you without pretence. You are the target of the powers of darkness and will have no rest until the God of peace will bruise the serpent's head under your feet.

2 TIMOTHY 2:3-4

"THOU THEREFORE ENDURE HARDNESS AS A GOOD SOLDIER OF JESUS CHRIST, NO MAN THAT WARRETH ENTANGLETH HIMSELF WITH THE AFFAIRS OF THIS LIFE, THAT HE MAY PLEASE HIM WHO HAS CHOSEN HIM TO BE A SOLDIER.

Jesus Christ to us ward is a testimony of temptation and long suffering, and as a master and lord in this field, we must learn to follow his steps in other to overcome our temptations. His key is humility and willingness to obey God's command and as wise as the oldest man, he uses the anointing of the Holy Spirit to put the power of the enemy under feet. He has commanded us to follow this divine law, to overcome the adversaries and tarry in faith, until he comes to give us our crown.

MATTHEW 10:16

"BEHOLD, I SEND YOU FORTH AS SHEEP IN THE MIDST OF WOLVES, BE YE THEREFORE WISE AS SERPENT, AND HARMLESS AS DOVES.

The lord has given us an assurance of defeat against Satan, if our obedience is fulfilled. Do that which is good and righteous, our God will put the powers of your enemies under your feet forever.

ROMANS 16:19-20

"FOR YOUR OBEDIENCE IS COME ABROAD UNTO ALL MEN. I AM GLAD THEREFORE ON YOUR BEHALF, BUT I WOULD HAVE YOU WISE UNTO THAT WHICH IS GOOD AND SIMPLE CONCERNING EVIL.

AND THE GOD OF PEACE SHALL BRUISE SATAN UNDER YOUR FEET SHORTLY, THE GRACE OF OUR LORD JESUS CHRIST BE WITH YOU AMEN. AMEN.

Apostle Paul has laid a foundation of the new covenant for the children of God and servant of God to obey and redeem with faith.

ROMAN 8:36

"WHO SHALL SEPARATE US FROM THE LOVE OF CHRIST? SHALL TRIBULATION OR DISTRESS OR PERSECUTION, OR FAMINE, OR NAKEDNESS, OR PERIL, OR SWORD? AS IT IS WRITTEN, FOR THY SAKE WE ARE KILLED ALL THE DAY LONG, WE ARE ACCOUNTED AS SHEEP FOR SLAUGHTER.

GOING THROUGH
THE WILDERNESS

DEUTERONOMY 8:2, 15, 16

"AND THOU SHALL REMEMBER ALL THE WAY WHICH THE LORD THY GOD, LED THEE THESE FORTY YEARS IN THE WILDERNESS, TO HUMBLE THEE AND TO PROVE THEE, TO KNOW WHAT WAS IN THINE HEART, WHETHER THOU WOULDEST KEEP HIS COMMANDMENT OR NOT.

WHO LED THEE THROUGH THIS GREAT AND TERRIBLE WILDERNESS, WHEREIN WHERE FEIRY SERPENT AND SCORPION, AND DROUGHT, WHERE THERE WAS NO WATER, WHO BROUGHT THEE FORTH WATER OUT OF THE ROCK OF FLINT.

WHO FED THEE IN THE WILDERNESS WITH MANNA, WHICH THY FATHER KNEW NOT, THAT HE MIGHT HUMBLE THEE, AND THAT HE MIGHT PROVE THEE, TO DO THEE GOOD AT THY LATTER END?

God's promise to Abraham is a promise to the Jews and Gentiles by faith. God's covenant and blessing to Abraham is for the children of God by faith. We are the children of Promise, the call, the chosen and the faithful. Every child of God must go through the course of freedom, the wilderness to reach our promise land. All children of promise has a land to possess, to possess the land we have a course to undergo, to prove to our father the almighty God that we are worthy to possess the land. It is a covenant between God and Abraham that his Children will suffer under bondage in Egypt and then go through the wilderness, before freedom forever. It becomes obvious that all covenant children of God must tread through this part to regain freedom. Jerusalem today which is the land of Canaan the promise land, is a symbolic of new Jerusalem which will emerge from heaven as the bible foretold, it is a land of eternal life to them that become the chosen. God revealed this to Jacob in a dream, when he was in his own course through the wilderness to Haran.

GENESIS 28:12,13,16,17

"AND HE DREAMED, AND BEHOLD A LADDER SET UP ON THE EARTH, AND THE TOP OF IT REACHED TO HEAVEN, AND BEHOLD THE ANGELS OF GOD ASCENDED AND DESCENDED UNTO IT.

AND BEHOLD, THE LORD STOOD ABOVE IT AND SAID, I AM THE LORD GOD OF ABRAHAM THY FATHER, AND THE GOD OF ISAAC, THE LAND WHERE ON THOU LAYEST, TO THEE WILL I GIVE IT AND TO THY SEEDS.

AND BEHOLD, I AM WITH THEE AND WILL KEEP THEE IN ALL PLACES, WITHER THOU GOEST, AND WILL BRING THEE AGAIN INTO THIS LAND, FOR I WILL NOT LEAVE THEE UNTIL I HAVE DONE THAT WHICH I HAVE SPOKEN TO THEE OF,

AND JACOB AWAKENED OF HIS SLEEP, AND HE SAID, SURELY THE LORD IS IN THIS PLACE, AND I KNEW IT NOT.

AND HE WAS AFRAID AND SAID, HOW DREADFUL IS THIS PLACE, THIS IS NON OTHER THAN THE

HOUSE OF GOD, AND THIS IS THE GATE OF HEAVEN.

Today the kingdom of God is a land to possess by the children of God. We are the children of promise and have our father's kingdom to possess, though the enemy may hinder, but God will give us victory, only we have to move on to the righteous side with God. Those that fellowship with Jesus Christ will certainly have the world to contend with which is our wilderness of today. Satan who is the prince of the world will afflict you with all sorrow, to make you be weary of the promise of God and probably back out or backslide from the faith and truth of the word. He will unleash on you wickedness in high places, serpents and scorpions against your flesh, drought and hunger against your survival, all this is for you to murmur and complain against God or tempt God as the children of God did in the wilderness, and was consumed by fire and serpent. But our God always told us to obey his word, as Jesus obeyed in his own wilderness and could not eat the bread of sorrow. God's word to us is to be patient in the lord, perseverance in tribulation, keep in the faith of Christ, do not be weary neither faint, for in a matter of time, you shall reap the fruit of joy.

GALATIANS 4:26, 28, 29,

"BUT JERUSALEM WHICH IS ABOVE IS FREE, WHICH IS THE MOTHER OF US ALL.

NOW WE BRETHREN, AS ISAAC WAS, ARE CHILDREN OF PROMISE.

BUT AS THEN HE THAT IS BORN AFTER THE FLESH PERSECUTED HIM THAT WAS BORN IN THE SPIRIT EVEN SO IT IS NOW.

No land or kingdom was promised to Ishmael neither Esau, because they were not chosen by God. But land and kingdom, was promised to Isaac and Jacob, because they are the chosen of God. Likewise you child of God, you are chosen and have a land to possess, which is the heavenly treasure.

THE OLD AND NEW WINE

MATTHEW 9:16-17

"NO MAN PUTETH A PIECE OF NEW CLOTH UNTO AN OLD GARMENT, FOR THAT WHICH IS PUT IN TO FILL IT UP, TAKETH FROM THE GARMENT, AND THE RENT IS MADE WORSE.

NEITHER DO MEN PUT NEW WINE INTO OLD BOTTLES, ELSE THE BOTTLE BREAKS, AND THE WINE RUNETH OUT, AND THE BOTTLE PERISH, BUT THEY PUT NEW WINE INTO NEW BOTTLES, NOR ARE BOTH PRESERVED.

The old wine defends the Law of Moses and commandment given in Mount Sinai, the holy mountain of God. It speaks of the blood of animal lamb of freedom. The children of God then are expected to honour and obey strictly to the laws of Moses given by God, the laws, covenant, ordinances, and statutes. But the generation of Moses was unable to keep to Gods commandment because the human nature erre. Even though God knows the attitude of human kind as unfaithful that he made provision for a sacrificial lamb to remit their sins. But day by day their disobedience grew worse and became a temptation to God that out of anger God consumed them with fire, and fiery serpent. But it repented of God not to continue with fury and anger against his children, that he sorted for a perfect way to redeem man from his disobedient state. For the reason of making relationship with God and man perfect, God considered animal sacrifice and man's effort to keep the commandment as imperfect. For man and his sacrifice could not satisfy the wants of God that he sought for the precious blood of human sacrifice which will bring perfection to his relationship with man. He gave his only son Jesus Christ to be the sacrificial lamb to bring perfection to God and man's relationship.

HEBREW 10:4, 5, 6, 9

"FOR IT IS NOT POSSIBLE THAT THE BLOOD OF GOATS AND BULLS SHOULD TAKE AWAY SINS.

WHEREFORE WHEN HE COMETH INTO THE WORLD, HE SAITH, SACRIFICE AND OFFERING THOU WOULDEST NOT, BUT A BODY HAS THOU PREFERED ME.

IN BURNT OFFERING AND SACRIFICE FOR SIN, THOU HAST HAD PLEASURE,

THEN SAID HE, LO, I COME TO DO THY WILL, O GOD. HE TAKETH THE FIRST THAT HE MAY ESTABLISH THE SECOND.

Jesus Christ of Nazareth show cased his ministry as the mediator of better covenant when he perform his first miracle by turning water into wine, to prove to the people of the world, that the second covenant shall be better, than the first covenant; the old and new wine.

JOHN 2:9-10

"WHEN THE RULER OF THE FEAST HAD TASTED THE WATER THAT WAS MADE WINE, AND KNEW NOT WHENCE IT COMES FROM, BUT THE SERVANTS WHICH DREW THE WATER KNEW THE GOVERNOR OF THE FEAST CALLED THE BRIDEGROOM,

AND SAITH UNTO HIM, EVERY MAN AT THE BEGINNING DOTH SET FORTH GOOD WINE, AND WHEN MAN HATH HAVE WELL DRUNK, THEN

*THAT WHICH IS WORSE, BUT THOU HAST KEPT
THE GOOD WINE UNTIL NOW.*

Christ came not to destroy the law, but to bring it to fulfilment as the bible recorded. The bible said the saviour will come to make the ways of man perfect to God, and that was the fulfilment of the law of the prophet, as Christ came as the saviour of the world. And has made our ways perfect to God by his body he sacrificed on the Calvary and the blood he shed to remit our sins. Every born again child of God is a child of the new covenant and New Testament in the blood of Jesus. Even as the Holy Spirit gave utterance to the men of the Jews to speak what they do not know about, spiritually confirming the mystery of the new wine, the power of the Holy Spirit.

ACTS 2:11-13

*"CRETES AND ARABIANS, WE DO HEAR THEM
SPEAK IN OUR TONGUES, THE WONDERFUL
WORKS OF GOD.*

*AND THEY WERE ALL AMAZED, AND WERE IN
DOUBT, SAYING ONE TO THE OTHER, WHAT
MANNER IS THIS?*

*OTHERS MOCKING SAID, THIS MEN ARE FULL OF
NEW WINE.*

The Pentecostal experience is the new wine, the mystery of the Holy Ghost to the children of God. Today the power of the Holy Spirit has become a strong power of intoxication, to the children of God. The glory of the latter house shall be greater than the former; we are of the new wine, the covenant in the blood of Jesus.

THE HOUR COMETH
AND NOW IS

JOHN 4:20-24

"OUR FATHER WORSHIPPED IN THIS MOUTAIN, AND YE SAY, THAT IN JERUSALEM IS THE PLACE WHERE MEN OUGHT TO WORSHIP.

JESUS SAITH UNTO HER, WOMAN, BELIEVE ME, THE HOUR COMETH, WHEN YE SHALL NEITHER IN THIS MOUNTAIN, NOR YET AT JERUSALEM, WORSHIP THE FATHER,

YE WORSHIP YE KNOW NOT WHAT; WE KNOW WHAT WE WORSHIP, FOR SALVATION IS OF THE JEWS.

BUT THE HOUR COMETH AND NOW IS, WHEN THE TRUE WORSHIPPERS SHALL WORSHIP THE FATHER IN SPIRIT AND IN TRUTH, FOR THE FATHER SEEKETH SUCH TO WORSHIP HIM. GOD IS A SPIRIT AND THOSE THAT WORSHIP HIM SHALL WORSHIP HIM IN SPIRIT AND IN TRUTH.

This Godless generation have dwelt much on this mountain in the name of worship, the world have compassed much on the old time religion that it becomes an abhor to God. God has asked us for a long time to move out from this mountain to the direction towards achieving or possessing the land of promise. Our God has left the mountain and cannot be pleased by mountain worship. God has sent his son for a new covenant and his son sent the Holy Ghost to us, since then the Holy Spirit has transformed the worship of God from religion to Christianity; meaning serving the lord in spirit and in truth, and crucifying the flesh as the lord did on the Calvary. It is an old fashion to serve our God in the flesh, because he does not live in the flesh, but he lives in the spirit. He planted his word in our spirit and expected it to bear fruit in the spirit.

DEUTRONOMY 1:6-8

"THE LORD OUR GOD SPAKE UNTO US IN HOREB SAYING YE HAVE DWELT LONG ENOUGH IN THIS MOUNT,

TURN YOU AND TAKE YOUR JOURNEY AND GO TO THE MOUNT OF THE AMORITES AND UNTO ALL THE PLACES NIGH THEREUNTO IN THE PLANE, IN THE HILLS, AND IN THE VALE AND IN THE SOUTH AND BY THE SEA SIDE, TO THE LAND OF THE CANNANITES AND UNTO LEBANON, UNTO THE GREAT RIVER, THE RIVER EUPHRATES,

BEHOLD, I HAVE SET THE LAND BEFORE YOU, GO IN AND POSSESS THE LAND WHICH THE LORD SWEAR UNTO YOUR FATHERS, ABRAHAM, ISAAC, AND JACOB TO GIVE UNTO THEM AND TO THEIR SEED AFTER THEM.

Our lord expects us to possess the land of promise which is the kingdom of God, not by law or effort of the flesh, but by the power of the Holy Spirit, which work in our spirit to accomplish every good work.

ROMAN 8:8-9

"SO THEN THEY THAT ARE IN THE FLESH CANNOT PLEASE GOD, BUT YE ARE NOT IN THE FLESH, BUT IN THE SPIRIT, IF SO BE THAT THE

SPIRIT OF GOD, DWELL IN YOU. NOW IF ANY MAN HAS NOT THE SPIRIT OF CHRIST, HE IS NONE OF HIS.

It would be very interesting to tell you men of the earth that the hour has come and now is, the time for Pentecostal dispensation. The age of explosion of power of the Holy Ghost, in demonstration, of power of God, in manifestation of gifts in mighty work and perfection. There is no time left for the routine, and cardinal laws of morning and evening mass, but the gathering of his people unto fellowship in the spirit of the lord. The spirit of the living God is in all children of God and our spirit is fertile to bear good fruit, if we honour the power of the Holy Spirit. We are expected to indwell in the well of salvation, a place of holiness, a habitual place of the Holy Spirit, rendering effectual service to the lord in the great vineyard of our God. We are no more guided by the law but controlled by the spirit, and influenced by his power, that our behaviour and character may become strange to the natural man, who does not understand the gift of God in our life. Someone controlled by the spirit may come up with what people see as unusual behaviour, speaking in tongues, utterances, miracles, visions, and prophesies. To heaven it is a normal life but to people on earth, it is considered as abnormal or spirit of fanaticism.

1 CORINTHIANS 2:14-15

"BUT THE NATURAL MAN RECIEVETH NOT THE THINGS OF THE SPIRIT, FOR THEY ARE FOOLISHNESS UNTO HIM, NEITHER CAN HE KNOW THEM, BECAUSE THEY ARE SPIRITUALLY DISERNED.

BUT HE THAT IS SPIRITUALLY JUDGED, ALL THINGS YET HE HIMSELF IS JUDGED OF NO MAN.

For those who believe in Christ, believe in his spirit and are children of rebirth, the born again, the adopted Children of God. For the sake of fruit of the spirit, we have no confidence in the flesh, and worship not God in flesh but glory in the spirit for righteousness sake.

PHILIPPIANS 3:2-3

"BEWARE OF DOGS, BEWARE OF EVIL WORKERS, BEWARE OF THE CONCISSION, FOR WE ARE THE CIRCUMCISION WHICH SERVE GOD IN THE SPIRIT AND REJOICE IN JESUS CHRIST, AND HAVE NO CONFIDENCE IN THE FLESH.

HE MUST INCREASE

ISAIAH 9:7

"OF THE INCREASE OF HIS GOVERNMENT AND PEACE, THERE SHALL BE NO END, UPON THE THRONE OF DAVID, AND UPON HIS KINGDOM, TO ORDER IT AND TO ESTABLISH IT WITH JUDGEMENT, AND WITH JUSTICE FROM HENCEFORTH, EVEN FOR EVER, THE ZEAL OF THE LORD OF HOST WILL PERFORM THIS.

Jesus Christ with the spirit of increase came to change the former things and to increase with the latter day's glory. All that came before him decreased, because a throne of increase was not appointed unto them and the ones that did not speak on his behalf, they came in through the back door. The increase of his government was prophesied by the prophets of old and since then Satan has laid a trap to destroy him and his ministry. But Jesus knowing this by the power of the Holy Spirit spoke forth through utterance of the Holy Ghost that his mission on earth is unstoppable, he has come to increase and fill the earth, with eternal gospel of truth and light.

JOHN 2:19

"JESUS ANSWERED AND SAID UNTO THEM,

DESTROY THIS TEMPLE AND IN THREE DAYS, I WILL RAISE IT UP.

This was proven when he died on the Calvary, in three days he built the temple of his body again to the shame of the prince of the world, Jesus is alive forever.

Adam and Eve came and decreased because they lacked the spirit of glory and wisdom, John the Baptist came and decreased because he was not given the spirit of glory, which is the spirit of increase but rather he was given the spirit of power and authority to preach and make way for the entrance of the lord's coming. Even as he baptized with water alone and not with spirit, confirms it all according to him that he who comes from above is above all.

JOHN 3:30-31

"HE MUST INCREASE BUT I MUST DECREASE.

HE THAT COMETH FROM ABOVE IS ABOVE ALL, HE THAT IS OF THE EARTH IS EARTHLY, AND SPEAKETH OF THE EARTH, HE THAT COMETH FROM HEAVEN IS ABOVE ALL.

Jesus Christ came to excel in honour and glory because it belongs to him alone. When he died and the world thought in the human understanding that all is ended, but to their astonishment and amazement his disciples rekindled their spirit to go on bearing witness for him, convincing the world that he is alive and would never cease to exist forever. He sent them to the gentiles and to the utmost part of the world to spread the news of the gospel. Today the apostolic gospel foundation is spreading and planting the word of God in every nook and cranny of the world with the power of the Holy Ghost, empowering the missionaries to preach the gospel to all nations.

MARK 16:14-15

"AFTER THAT HE APPEARED UNTO THE ELEVEN WHO SAT AT MEAT, AND UPBRAIDED THEM WITH THEIR UNBELIEF AND HEARDNESS OF HEART, BECAUSE THEY BELIEVE NOT THEM

WHICH HAD SEEN HIM AFTER HE WAS RISEN. AND HE SAID UNTO THEM, GO YE UNTO THE WORLD, AND PREACH THE GOSPEL TO EVERY CREATURE.

The glory of the latter house shall be greater than the former, his fame, glory and honour will continue to overcome the world, because he has come to give glory to them that believe that he is the king of glory. But those who came from the back door with false religion and message must decrease because they speak of the earth and has in them spirit of decrease. An American renowned musician, played a song which says that the name of Jesus will cease to exist in a couple of years. Though he is late, there is an evidence today that the name Jesus has become a household name in every cranny and nook corner of the world. He who blaspheme has his portion in hell fire as the word of God told us. The cup of the wicked is fire and brimstone, because he blasphemed.

PSALM 9:16-17

"THE LORD IS KNOWN BY THE JUDGEMENT WHICH HE EXECUTETH, THE WICKED IS SNARED IN THE WORK OF HIS OWN HANDS, HIGGAION SELAH

THE WICKED SHALL BE TURNED INTO HELL, AND ALL THE NATIONS THAT FORGET GOD.

So it shall be to every occult church, religion and every false prophet of the world. But the gates of hell shall not prevail against the church of God; the church of God must match on.

MATTHEW 16:18

"AND I SAY UNTO THEE, THAT THOU ART PETER, AND UPON THE ROCK, I WILL BUILD MY CHURCH, AND THE GATE OF HELL SHALL NOT PREVAIL AGAINST IT.

The God of true Christianity is the God of increase, who will continue to multiply the children of God in manifold and multiple fold. His kingdom has no end, heaven and earth all belong to the great **ACIENT OF DAYS**.

LUKE 1:33

"AND HE SHALL REIGN OVER THE HOUSE OF JACOB FOR EVER, AND OF HIS KINGDOM THEIR SHALL BE NO END.

THE WELL OF SALVATION

ISAIAH 12:1-3

"AND IN THAT DAY THOU SHALL SAY, O LORD, I WILL PRAISE YOU, THOUGH THOU WAST ANGRY WITH ME, THINE ANGER IS TURNED AWAY, AND THOU COMFORTEST ME.

BEHOLD GOD IS MY SALVATION, I WILL TRUST AND NOT BE AFRAID, FOR THE LORD JEHOVAH IS MY STRENTH, AND MY SONG HE ALSO IS BECOME MY SALVATION.

THEREFORE WITH JOY SHALL YE DRAW WATER OUT OF THE WELLS OF SALVATION.

In common understanding salvation means to save from danger. But in the bible context salvation means saving one from the danger of devil and translating such one into the kingdom of God. In another interpretation, it means redeeming someone from the power of the darkness, through the power of the Holy Spirit, and transforming such one into the marvellous light of Jesus. The word of God says there is no other salvation except through our lord Jesus Christ. He is the horn of salvation; power of our salvation, and the one that establishes it.

LUKE 1:68-69

"BLESSED BE THE GOD OF ISREAL, FOR HE HAS VISITED AND REDEEMED HIS PEOPLE.

*AND HAS RAISE UP OUR HORN OF SALVATION
FOR US IN THE HOUSE OF HIS SERVANT DAVID.*

In divine language, the well of salvation means the dwelling or the inhabitable stream of the righteous, where the power of light and glory radiate. The Holy Spirit is the power that controls the well and preserves it for holiness for the consumption of the soul of eternal life. It is a well of chariot of grace and anointing, where the Holy Spirit ordain the righteous with auction of anointing in diverse gifts of power. When you indwell in the well of salvation you are righteous, you are in the light of Jesus and his glory overshadows you, the word of God abides in you and his glory indwells in you. You are a true child of God, and of the spirit of freedom and glory.

2 CORINTHIANS 3:17-18

"NOW THE LORD IS THAT SPIRIT, AND WHERE THE SPIRIT OF THE LORD LIVES THERE IS LIBERTY.

BUT WE ALL WITH OPEN FACE BEHOLDING US IN A GLASS THE GLORY OF THE LORD ARE CHANGED INTO THE SAME IMAGE FROM GLORY TO GLORY EVEN AS BY THE SPIRIT OF THE LORD.

Those who abide in this well abide in the power of the Holy Spirit and have no confidence in the flesh, but trust in the spirit. Our anointing power, strength, virtue and all fruit of the spirit, comes from the spring well of salvation.

Jesus is the life giving water and has called all that thirst to come and drink in his well of life giving water, to preserve our life forever. The woman of Samaria demanded to drink this water if Jesus could give her. What about you mortal man? Wouldn't you like to live a life of immortality? If you would sustain your life in a life giving water in a well of salvation.

JOHN 4:14

"BUT WHOSEVER DRINKETH OF THE WATER, THAT I SHALL GIVE HIM, SHALL NEVER THIRST. BUT THE WATER THAT I SHALL GIVE HIM, SHALL BE IN HIM A WELL OF SPRINGING UP INTO EVERLASTING LIFE.

THE SEAL OF THE HOLY SPIRIT OF PROMISE

EPHESIANS 1:13-14

"IN WHOM YE ALSO TRUSTED, AFTER

THAT YE HEARD THE WORD OF TRUTH, THE GOSPEL OF YOUR SALVATION, IN WHOM ALSO AFTER THAT YE BELIEVED, YE WERE SEALED WITH THAT HOLY SPIRIT OF PROMISE.

WHICH IS THE EARNEST OF OUR INHERITANCE, UNTIL THE REDEMPTION OF THE PURCHASED POSSESSION, UNTO THE PRAISE OF HIS GLORY?

To them that God predestinate to be his children in the image of his son Jesus Christ, Jesus in his authority will justify them by washing of water and blood, and rightfully become their personal saviour and lord. In turn the Holy Ghost will sanctify the believers, by anointing them with power to become the children of God. The Holy Spirit will preserve them in his well of salvation, by indwelling in them, glorifying their body as a temple of God and glory. Therefore the seal of the holy spirit of promise is the anointing of glory and power by the Holy Spirit to the children of God. He is the comforter our father promised through Jesus Christ to send to us to ordain all things to our good and understanding.

JOHN 14:17

"EVEN THE SPIRIT OF TRUTH, WHOM THE WORLD CANNOT RECEIVE, BECAUSE IT SEETH HIM NOT, NEITHER KNOWETH HIM, BUT YE KNOW HIM FOR HE DWELLETH WITH YOU AND SHALL BE IN YOU.

When a child is born in the kingdom of God by adoption, in the day of his ritual cleansing by water and blood, called the immersion baptism, the Holy Spirit will put a stamp of seal of power. The seal of the Father, seal of the Son, and seal of the Holy Spirit, to make his work a perfect work of the holy trinity. He is the perfect work force to ordain all works of God to a glory seal. In the day of sanctification of every child of God by the power of the Holy Spirit, there shall be transformation or renewal of life in the body and the spirit of the child of God. It is a process of the removal of the unwanted in the life of the believer. Firstly, darkness and lies shall be a cast away in the believer's life, light and truth shall take their place thereby establishing in the believer a manifest of power and glory by the seal of the Holy Spirit.

1 JOHN 5:6-8

"THIS IS HE THAT CAME BY WATER AND BLOOD, EVEN JESUS CHRIST, NOT BY WATER ONLY BUY BY WATER AND BLOOD, AND IT IS THE SPIRIT THAT BEARETH WITNESS BECAUSE THE SPIRIT IS TRUTH.

FOR THERE ARE THREE THAT BEAR RECORD IN HEAVEN, THE FATHER, THE SON AND THE HOLY GHOST, AND THESE THREE ARE ONE.

AND THERE ARE THREE THAT BEAR WITNESS IN EARTH, THE SPIRIT AND THE WATER AND THE BLOOD, AND THESE THREE AGREE IN ONE.

As the child of God grow in the Lord, the Holy Spirit will anoint him with chariots of Grace of the Lord, to serve the lord in all good work and manner, with auctions of His anointing for effectual service to the Lord.

EPHESIANS 4:7

"BUT UNTO EVERY ONE OF US IS GIVEN GRACE, ACCORDING TO THE MEASURE OF THE GIFT OF CHRIST.

The life of every believer is plugged into the socket of the Holy Spirit. We receive our spiritual light, insight to all works of our life from the power of the Holy Spirit. He influences us, controls us, and directs us to the will of God. It is impossible for a child of God to ignore the Holy Spirit, and maintain his spiritual force. Any act of carelessness to the Holy Spirit will grieve the spirit, and will be considered as ingratitude to the marvellous work he has done for us

EPHESIANS 4:30

"AND GREIVE NOT THE HOLY SPIRIT OF GOD, WHEREBY YE ARE SEALED UNTO THE DAY OF REDEMPTION.

COMETH HE IN LIKE MANNER

ACT 1:10-11

"AND WHILE THEY LOOKED STEADFASTLY TOWARDS HEAVEN AS HE WENT UP, BEHOLD TWO MEN STOOD BY THEM IN WHITE APPAREL,

WHICH ALSO SAID, YE MEN OF GALILEE, WHY STAND YE GAZING UP INTO HEAVEN? THIS SAME JESUS WHICH IS TAKEN UP FROM YOU INTO HEAVEN SHALL SO COME IN LIKE MANNER AS YOU HAS SEEN HIM GO INTO HEAVEN.

The words of God said for them that believe receive, and those who do not believe will not receive. The testimony of our lord Jesus Christ is the spirit of prophesy. The coming of the messiah was prophesied by the prophets of old, and the messiah came as foretold; Emmanuel who was Baptised to be Jesus Christ of Nazareth. He came for the purpose of setting man free from the bondage of eternal death and this he accomplished by his death on the calvary. He is preparing also to come again as the prophesy also told us. How prepared are you in wait for the lord? The word of God said Heaven and Earth shall pass away but my word shall not pass away. Every word of God must not return to him void, but must prosper and accomplish in the things he sent it forth.

HABAKKUK 2:2-3

WRITE THE VISION AND MAKE IT PLAIN UPON TABLES THAT HE MAY RUN THAT READETH IT

*FOR THE VISION IS YET FOR AN APPOINTED TIME,
BUT AT THE END IT SHALL SPEAK AND NOT LIE,
THOUGH IT TARRY WAIT FOR IT, BECAUSE IT
WILL SURELY COME, IT WILL NOT TARRY.*

The purpose for the first coming has been accomplished as prophesied; the second shall also be fulfilled in like manner. Our lord said the purpose for the second coming is to gather the saints, to bring glory in his saints, to judge the world, to reign, to receive us to himself and to destroy death everlasting. He is the God of truth and will accomplish the truth that is in him; His word is that the just shall leave by faith. The Bible said that his second coming shall be in two stages; the rapture and the millennium. The rapture which he will come in secret to take the saints, the dead and the alive in saint shall be caught up with him in the air as he come in glory with the angels.

1 THESSALONIANS 4:14-17

*"FOR IF WE BELIEVE THAT JESUS DIED AND ROSE
AGAIN, EVEN SO THEM ALSO WHICH SLEEP IN
JESUS WILL GOD BRING WITH HIM.*

*FOR THIS WE SAY UNTO YOU BY THE WORD OF
THE LORD, THAT WE WHICH ARE ALIVE AND
REMAIN UNTO THE COMING OF THE LORD
SHALL NOT PREVENT THEM WHICH ARE ASLEEP.*

*FOR THE LORD HIMSELF SHALL DESCEND FROM
HEAVEN WITH A SHOUT, WITH THE VOICE OF
THE ARCH ANGEL, AND WITH THE TRUMP OF
GOD, AND THE DEAD IN CHRIST SHALL RISE
FIRST.*

*THEN WE WHICH ARE ALIVE SHALL BE CAUGHT
UP WITH THEM IN THE CLOUD, TO MEET THE
LORD IN THE AIR, AND SO SHALL WE BE WITH
THE LORD.*

WHEREFORE COMFORT ONE ANOTHER WITH THESE WORDS.

Christ shall come to set up the millennium with the saints. This time Christ and the saints shall be set to judge the word. The goat and the sheep shall be separated, and each in their designated kingdom. Christ and the saints shall reign for one thousand years during which all curses upon the earth shall be removed.

1 THESSALONIANS 3:13

"TO THE END HE MAY STABLISH YOUR HEART, UNBLAMEABLE IN HOLINESS BEFORE GOD, EVEN OUR FATHER AT THE COMING OF OUR LORD JESUS CHRIST WITH ALL HIS SAINTS.

Shall we continue to doubt as Thomas did or shall we live by faith? Be not the soul that draw back into perdition, but believe in the truth, the saving of soul is the wisdom of a true son of God.

THE JUST SHALL LIVE BY FAITH

HEBREW 10:37-39

"FOR YET A LITTLE WHILE AND HE SHALL COME, WILL COME AND WILL NOT TARRY.

NOW THE JUST SHALL LIVE BY FAITH, BUT IF ANY MAN DRAW BACK, MY SOUL SHALL HAVE NO PLEASURE IN HIM.

BUT WE ARE NOT OF THEM WHO DRAW BACK INTO PERDITION, BUT OF THEM THAT BELIEVE TO THE SAVING OF THE SOUL.

No one has ever seen God except his son Jesus Christ, who came and lived among us, who told the just to live by faith, to receive the things of God and heaven. God has revealed himself in righteousness from faith to faith, he is a faithful father and expects us to receive and know him by faith in our spirit. God indwell in the light that eye cannot see, so it is impossible to see God with human eyes, even Moses that God revealed part of his body to, his face became dazzled that no one looked at his face, he had to cover his face with veil. This is the more reason why God decided to permit his spirit to live in us, so that we could feel his presence always, and know God is with us and live in us.

1 TIMOTHY 6:16

"WHO ONLY HAD IMMORTALITY DWELLING IN THE LIGHT WHICH NO MAN CAN APPROACH

UNTO, WHOM NO MAN HATH SEEN, NOR CAN SEE, TO WHOM BE HONOR AND POWER, AMEN.

God made it plain to Moses that no man can see him and live, God made us to know who he is through our lord Jesus Christ, and Jesus also established his presence by giving us the Holy Spirit. We are living in the era of the new covenant where we serve and worship God by faith and receive him by faith, so as to please our maker. Without faith we cannot please God. He is Ominipresence everywhere and everything in our life. Faith is the strength to reach heaven and the key to silence the travail of the world, so the just must live by faith to achieve a victorious end or life.

EXODUS 33:20

AND HE SAID, THOU CANST NOT SEE MY FACE FOR THERE SHALL NO MAN SEE ME AND LIVE

If we have the believe that God live, that Jesus is alive and the Holy Spirit is present in us, we have established faith in God. We worship God not to open our eyes to see him but to be rest assured that where ever we gather in the name of our lord Jesus, God is with us, he has an open ear to hear our prayers and answer our entire request. It is by faith that the children of God reached the Promised Land. No one can worship God without faith and please him, but when you know God by faith and receive him by faith, you will please him and he will reward your faithfulness.

HEBREW 11:6

"BUT WITHOUT FAITH IT IS IMPOSSIBLE TO PLEASE HIM, FOR HE THAT COMETH TO GOD MUST BELIEVE THAT HE IS, AND THAT HE IS A REWARDER OF THEM THAT DELIGENTLY SEEK HIM.

Today God reveals himself through the spirit, which speak for the father and the son. And no man has ever seen the spirit, but yet the spirit is everywhere in our life. Our faith in the lord is that which we have not seen but believe because we know it is the truth, and our believe is without a turning point. Jesus is the one that has seen the father, and we witness that he is the true son of God, as he is, so also his father is truthful and faithful.

JOHN 1:18

"NO MAN HATH SEEN GOD AT ANYTIME, EXCEPT THE ONLY BEGOTTEN SON WHICH IS IN THE BOSSOM OF THE FATHER, HE HATH DECLARED HIM.

It is by faith we can do all things in the lord. With faith we war against principalities, believing that God is on our side, and our weapons is not of the flesh but mighty through God to the pulling down of strong holds. Our shield of faith quenches the fiery darts of the enemies.

PUT ON THE WHOLE ARMOR OF GOD

EPHESIANS 6:13:14

"WHEREFORE, TAKE UNTO YOU THE WHOLE ARMOR OF GOD, THAT YE MAY BE ABLE TO WITHSTAND IN THE EVIL DAY, AND HAVING DONE ALL TO STAND, STAND THEREFORE, HAVING YOUR LOINES GIRT ABOUT WITH TRUTH, AND HAVING ON THE BREAST PLATE OF RIGHTEOUSNESS.

The armour of God is the righteousness of God, and the righteousness of God is in the spirit, it does not abide in the flesh. The power of his might is the power in the spirit of man. Therefore, it is the spirit man that puts on the armour of God and not the natural man. Things of God are discerned spiritually, that the natural cannot benefit but the spiritual benefit. As a child of God, to put on the armour of God is to be righteous, and to be righteous is to obey the word of God, and his will over our life. Men of God or children of God need to keep their environment holy, by abiding in the power of righteousness which is Jesus, the vine of the vineyard. In this case, the Holy Spirit will empower you to bear the fruit of righteousness, which is the armour to destroy the spirit of the unrighteous.

2 CORINTHIANS 10:3-6

FOR THOUGH WE WALK IN THE FLESH, WE DO NOT WAR AFTER THE FLESH,

FOR WEAPONS OF OUR WELFARE ARE NOT CARNAL, BUT MIGHTY THROUGH GOD TO THE PULLING DOWN OF STRONG HOLDS

CASTING DOWN IMAGINATIONS AND EVERY STRONG THING THAT EXALTETH ITSELF AGAINST THE KNOWLEDE OF GOD, AND BRINGING WITH CAPTIVITY EVERY THOUGHT OF THE OBEDIENCE OF CHRIST.

AND HAVING IN A READINESS TO REVENGE ALL DISOBEDIENCE WHEN YOUR OBEDIENCE IS FULFILLED.

The disobedience of all that exalted itself against the knowledge of God can be revenged when your righteousness in God is fulfilled. Our righteousness is obeying the word of God, and the contents of righteousness are the spirit, truth and faith. To bear fruit in righteousness which is the armour of God is to have salvation which is light unto our soul, believing in truth which is the word of God and the shield of faith, which is confidence in God, automatically, this quenches the fiery dart of the enemy. The canal man cannot wear the armour of God, but the spiritual man is best suited. The canal man does not please God and cannot achieve righteousness, because he is of the earth and the earth speak of the flesh. But if Christ is in you, you have crucified the body because of sin and your spirit is alive because of righteousness. Then your obedience is fulfilled in God when you have the righteousness of God. The auction of anointing and power in you brings the power of the wicked to nought.

When your obedience is fulfilled in righteousness, your faith becomes a stronghold. Faith without work is death; you can put your faith to practice by applying fervent prayers, which is the weapon to quench the fiery darts of the wicked. The war is not of man but of God, and they are spiritually discerned.

EPHESIANS 6:18

"PRAYING ALWAYS WITH ALL PRAYER AND SUPPLICATION IN THE SPIRIT, AND WATCHING THEREUNTO WITH ALL PRESERVARANCE AND SUPPLICATION UNTO ALL SAINTS.

The weapon of warfare is fervent prayer, which burns like fuel of fire, which is a new battle covenant in the blood of Jesus.

ISAIAH 9:5-6

"FOR EVERY BATTLE OF THE WARRIOR IS WITH CONFUSED NOISE, AND GARMENTS ROLLED IN BLOOD, BUT THESE SHALL BE WITH BURNING AND FUEL OF FIRE.

FOR UNTO US A CHILD IS BORN, UNTO US A SON IS GIVEN, AND THE GOVERNMENT SHALL BE UPON HIS SHOULDERS AND HIS NAME SHALL BE CALLED WONDERFUL, COUNCELLOR, THE MIGHTY GOD, THE EVERLASTING FATHER, THE PRINCE OF PEACE.

Jesus is the new covenant of warfare, the armor that destroy by fire and not pull of blood any longer.

DESIRE THE SINCERE MILK OF THE WORD

1 PETER 2:2-3

"AS A NEW BORN BABY, DESIRE THE SINCERE MILK OF THE WORD, THAT YE MAY GROW THEREBY.

IF SO BE YE HAVE TASTED THAT THE LORD IS GRACIOUS.

As a born again child of God, desire the sincere milk of the word of God. Blessed are they who do hunger and thirst after righteousness for they shall be filled. When you truly from the depth of your heart desire to understand the word of God, a passage of understanding will be opened unto you. When you declare your spirit as poor in the knowledge of the word, the spirit of God will fill your spirit with great knowledge and understanding of the secret of the word. The bible said, desire the word like a new born baby which you are as a born again child of God. Give your attention to the Holy Spirit, He will nourish you with great wisdom in the word, and build a foundation of sound understanding in your life. From your willing heart always hunger to know the will of God which is a light to guide you in the part to the kingdom of God. Not puffed up with pride or proving to be paragon of knowledge, deceiving yourselves.

1 TIMOTHY 6:3-5

"IF ANY MAN TEACH OTHERWISE, AND CONSENT NOT TO WHOLESOME WORDS, EVEN THE WORD OF OUR LORD JESUS CHRIST, AND

TO THE DOCTRINGE WHICH IS ACCORDING TO GODLINESS,

HE IS PROUD, KNOWING NOTHING, BUT DOTING ABOUT QUESTIONS AND STRIFES OF WORDS, WHEREOF COMETH STRIFE, RAILING EVIL SURMISINGS.

PERVERSE DISPUTING OF MEN OF CORRUPT MINDS, AND DESTITUTE OF THE TRUTH, SUPPOSING THAT GAIN IS GODLINESS, FROM SUCH WITHDRAW THYSELF.

The word of God is spirit and truth, and need to be followed with sincere heart, submitting our spirit to the control of the Holy Spirit. Not with itching ears or tongue of argument but eager to learn in humility as babes. The word is not for the wise or prudent but to them which do not know, as they desire to know God will reveal it unto them, because of honesty and sincerity of heart.

2 TIMOTHY 3:14

"BUT CONTINUE THOU IN THE THINGS WHICH THOU HAST LEARNT AND HAST BEEN ASSURED OF, KNOWING OF WHOM THOU HAST LEARNED THEM.

AND THAT FROM A CHILD THOU HAST KNOWN THE SCRIPTURES, WHICH ARE ABLE TO MAKE THE WISE UNTO SALVATION, THROUGH FAITH WHICH IS IN JESUS CHRIST.

When you seek the word with faithfulness, the word will abide in you and bear fruit in you, the truth in the word will set you free, the light in the word will guide you through, and the glory of the word will make you a perfect child of God.

JOHN 8:31-32

"THEN SAID JESUS TO THOSE JEWS WHO BELIEVED IN HIM, IF YOU CONTINUE IN MY WORD, THEN ARE YE MY DISCIPLES INDEED, AND YE SHALL KNOW THE TRUTH AND THE TRUTH SHALL SET YOU FREE.

THE ENTRANCE OF THY WORDS GIVETH LIGHT AND UNDERSTANDING

EPHISIANS 1:17-19

THAT THE GOD OF OUR LORD JESUS CHRIST, THE FATHER OF GLORY, MAY GIVE UNTO YOU THE SPIRIT OF WISDOM AND REVELATION IN THE KNOWLEDGE OF HIM.

THE LIGHT OF YOUR UNDERSTANDING BEING UNDERSTANDING, THAT YE MAY KNOW WHAT IS THE HOPE OF HIS CALLING, AND WITH THE RICHES OF THE GLORY OF HIS INHERITANCE IN THE SAINTS.

AND WHAT IS THE EXCEEDING GREATNESS OF HIS POWER TO US WARD WHO BELIEVES, ACCORDING TO THE WORKING OF HIS MIGHTY POWER.

The total understanding of the knowledge of God is the light, the truth, and the spirit in the word. The spirit of the word of God shines light in the word and the truth of the word manifest understanding to the willing heart. Jesus is the word, the truth and the light, the truth in the word of God sets free the confused mind. The spirit of the word is the spirit of truth and light, it is the spirit that creates an entrance for understanding of the word of God by shinning the light to the heart of men for them to see the truth in the word. For every word of God, the Holy Spirit makes an entrance for understanding through the power of truth and light in the word, to the curious seekers. The Holy Spirit is a teacher and eager to make a channel of understanding to the humble and simple in mind. Every word of God speaks the truth and manifest light to the confused mind. The Holy Spirit makes a revelation through the word of God to the understanding of the simple about the ways of God, his mysterious nature, his divine attribute and His sovereign nature. God has created light and understanding in his word to remove fear, complexity and confusion in the mind of the believers.

2 PETER 1:11

"FOR SO AN ENTRANCE SHALL BE MINISTERED UNTO YOU, ABUNDANTLY INTO THE EVERLASTING KINGDOM OF OUR LORD AND SAVIOR JESUS CHRIST.

The circumcisions that worship God in spirit receive the spirit of knowledge and wisdom of the word. A passage of understanding is created by the Holy Spirit, for them through light and truth in the word, and they remain in the truth and the light. But the circumcision that worship God in the flesh, receive the wisdom of the flesh and are blinded, from the light and truth of the word, which came from the root of the prince of the world, and certainly they shall remain in perpetual darkness of the word.

2 CORINTHIANS 4:4-6

"IN WHOM THE GOD OF THIS WORD HATH BLINDED, THE MIND OF THEM WHICH BELIEVE NOT, LEST THE LIGHT OF THE GLORIOUS GOSPEL OF CHRIST, WHO IS THE IMAGE OF GOD, SHOULD SHINE UNTO THEM. FOR WHICH PREACH NOT OURSELVES, BUT CHRIST JESUS OUR LORD, AND OURSELVES YOUR SERVANTS FOR JESUS SAKE.

FOR GOD WHO COMMANDETH THE LIGHT TO SHINE OUT OF DARKNESS, HATH SHINE IN OUR HEARTS, TO GIVE THE LIGHT OF THE KNOWLEDGE OF THE GLORY OF GOD, IN THE FACE OF JESUS CHRIST.

Those who believe not receive not; the wisdom of man is foolishness to God. There are those who claim to know the secret things of God, but are standing in the dark, they do it out of conceit and emptiness. These are the occult religion setting, and the churches of delusion, who believe in acquiring knowledge out of philosophy and fables. The bible said that those who exalt themselves against the knowledge of God shall be brought to obedience, God shall bring them down to shame. The knowledge of the word is given to the babes in the lord, and not to the prudent and wise.

MATTHEW 11:25

"AT THAT TIME JESUS ANSWERED AND SAID, I THANK THEE O LORD, FATHER OF HEAVEN AND EARTH, BECAUSE THOU HAST HEED THESE THINGS FROM THE WISE AND PRUDENT, AND HAST REVEALED THEM UNTO BABES.

EVEN SO FATHER, FOR SO IT SEEMED GOOD IN THY SIGHT.

THE SPIRIT OF GOD IS UPON ME

ACT 1:8-9

"BUT YE SHALL RECEIVE POWER, AFTER THAT, THE HOLY GHOST IS COME UPON YOU, AND YE SHALL BE A WITNESS UNTO ME EVEN IN JERUSALEM, AND IN ALL JUDEA, AND IN SAMERIA, AND UNTO THE UTMOST PART OF THE EARTH.

AND WHEN HE HAS SPOKEN THESE THINGS, WHILE THEY BEHELD, HE WAS TAKEN UP, AND A CLOUD RECEIVED HIM OUT OF THEIR SIGHT.

We are the earthen vessels of God, not with emptiness but filled with the power of God to do exploit for the Lord. The lord released his gift, power and grace upon us to be effectual in his service, to them that believe, receive the promise. The power of the holy spirit of promise is upon every child of God and servants of God. We have treasure in the Holy Spirit, all we are required to do is activate the power of the spirit by action and actualize the mandate of God without impediment by influencing the world for Christ. The Bible says that God has not given us the spirit to fear but of power, love and sound mind, and greater is he that is in you than he that is in the world. In Jesus we are complete, who is the head of principalities and powers, and the ultimate of all powers. Those who know their God make great exploit of his power.

DANIEL 11:32

"AND SUCH AS DO WICKEDLY AGAINST THE COVENANT SHALL BE CORRUPT BY FLATTERIES, BUT THE PEOPLE THAT DO KNOW THEIR GOD, SHALL BE STRONG AND DO EXPLOIT.

Jesus Christ promised to give his spirit to all children of God, to empower them to be of spirit rather than flesh. To be aware of the power of God in them, to utilize the Holy Ghost power effectively in the vineyard of God. To everyone he called he gave the power to become the children of God, and to everyone he sent, he gave the power to accomplish the mission. Jesus said whoever shall believe and is baptized shall his signs follow, they shall perform miracles, signs and wonders. Whether you are called, chosen or faithful, the spirit of God is upon you. Let your faith be in action and at work, faith without work is dead.

MARK 16:17-18

AND THESE SIGNS SHALL FOLLOW THEM THAT BELIEVE IN MY NAME SHALL THEY CAST OUT DEVILS; THEY SHALL SPEAK WITH NEW TONGUES.

THEY SHALL TAKE UP SERPENTS, AND IF THEY DRINK ANY DEADLY THING, IT SHALL NOT HURT THEM, THEY SHALL LAY HANDS ON THE SICK, AND THEY SHALL RECOVER.

The apostles of Jesus Christ were aware of the anointing of the power of the Holy Spirit upon them, and they make effective use of the power, without waiting upon God to give them further instructions or permission to use the power. Unlike Moses who always asks God for permission before executing action on the power of God upon him, by so doing suffer in the means of abundance of power. But the apostles of Jesus Christ with chariots of grace of anointing made a great exploit of the power of God in them without giving the devil the chance to play on their intelligence;

because they know that he that is in them is greater than he that is in the world. Apostle Peter laid a foundation of ministry of the power of the Holy Spirit, the power in the tongue, the power to speak and it shall establish.

ACTS 3:4-8

"AND PETER FASTENING HIS EYES UPON HIM WITH JOHN SAID, LOOK AT US,

AND HE GAVE HEED UNTO THEM, EXPECTING TO RECEIVE SOMETHING FROM THEM.

THEN PETER SAID, SILVER AND GOLD HAVE I NONE, BUT SUCH AS I HAVE GAVE I UNTO THEE. IN THE NAME OF JESUS CHRIST OF NAZARETH, RISE UP AND WALK.

AND HE TOOK HIM BY THE RIGHT HAND AND LIFTED HIM UP, AND IMMEDIATELY, HIS KNEES AND ANKLES RECEIVED STRENGTH.

AND HE LEAPING UP STOOD AND WALKED OUT AND ENTERED WITH THEM INTO THE TEMPLE, WALKING AND LEAPING AND PRAISING GOD.

Brethren, you have God with you, who is above every other God and your God is the ultimate in power, exercise your faith and send out your power for a great work of God.

OCCUPY TILL I COME

LUKE 19:12-13

"HE SAID THEREFORE, A CERTAIN NOBLE MAN WENT INTO A FAR COUNTRY TO RECEIVE FOR HIMSELF, A KINGDOM, AND TO RETURN, AND HE CALLED HIS TEN SERVANTS, AND DELIVERED THEM TEN POUNDS, AND SAID UNTO THEM, OCCUPY TILL I COME.

The business of Jesus Christ our Raboni before he returned to heaven and sat at the right hand of His father, is to seek for the flocks of his father and to gather them unto fellowship with him, as it is written in the book of;

GENESIS 49:10

"THE SCEPTRE SHALL NOT DEPART FROM JUDAH NOR A LAW GIVER FROM BETWEEN HIS FEET UNTIL SHILOH COMES AND UNTO HIM SHALL THE GATHERING OF THE PEOPLE BE.

Jesus Christ is the sceptre of the tribe of Judah, and today it is unto him that the Christians gather together for fellowship. When he was ascending, he knew we have a glorious open door, but adversaries are abound, so he held captivity captive and released his gifts, grace and power unto children of God to equip them for work of the ministry to edify the church of God. This is for us to keep in his business of salvation till he comes as the salvation army of Christ.

EPHESIANS 4:7-8

"BUT UNTO EVERY ONE OF US IS GIVEN GRACE, ACCORDING TO THE MEASURE OF THE GIFT OF CHRIST.

WHEREFORE HE SAITH, WHEN HE ASCENDED UPON ON HIGH, HE LED CAPTIVITY CAPTIVE, AND GAVE GIFT UNTO MEN.

What you are to do, do it fast the night is far spent the day is at hand, the master may be here at any moment. Prepare your stewardship for the master's supervision; for whatever he has sent us to do he expects us to do it well and perfect. If you are sent as an evangelist do the work of your ministry, for there is a purpose for every gift of God on earth, and every one is a master in his own mission, according to grace of God.

2 TIMOTHY 4:5

"BUT WATCH THOU IN ALL THINGS ENDURE AFFLICTIONS, DO THE WORK OF AN EVANGELIST, MAKE FULL PROOF OF THY MINISTRY.

The shepherds he also charged to feed his flocks as he told peter to feed his flocks. He instructed the pastors to feed the flocks, to plant their feet perfect in the house of God, to keep them abiding for the kingdom sake, waiting patiently for his coming. Those that prophesy should prophesy wisely according to the grace of utterance given by the Holy Spirit. Teachers should teach according to the measure of grace given and every other gift should be at work to edify the work of God.

ROMANS 12:1-8

"SO WE BEING MANY, ARE ONE BODY IN CHRIST, AND EVERYONE MEMBERS ONE OF ANOTHER. HAVING THEN GIFTS, DIFFERING ACCORDING TO THE GRACE THAT IS GIVEN TO US, WHETHER

PROPHESY, LET US PROPHESY ACCORDING TO THE PROPORTION OF FAITH.

OR MINISTRY, LET US WAIT ON OUR MINISTERING, OR THAT TEACHETH ON TEACHING.

OR HE THAT EXORTETH, ON EXORTATION, HE THAT GIVETH LET HIM DO IT WITH SIMPLICITY, HE THAT RULETH WITH DILIGENCE, HE THAT SHOWETH MERCY WITH CHEERFULNESS.

UNTO JUDAH SHALL THE GATHERING OF HIS PEOPLE BE

GENESIS 49:10

"THE SCEPTRE SHALL NOT DEPART FROM JUDAH, NOR A LAW GIVER FROM BETWEEN HIS FEET, UNTIL SHILOH CAME, AND UNTO HIM SHALL THE GATHERING OF HIS PEOPLE BE.

Almighty God has anointed and ordained Jesus Christ of Nazareth, the lion of the tribe of Judah, the Sceptre that saved the world, that unto him shall the people of God gather. Even as the church in heaven so also shall the church on earth fellowship unto him who is the all and all, the head of sanctified churches. The bible has told us the children of God, those who believed in Christ not to forsake the habit of assembling together as one in the lord, and most of all for us to be renewed in the strength of God daily, this is for the earnest hope of his coming.

HEBREW 10:25

"NOT FORSAKING THE ASSEMBLING OF OURSELVES TOGETHER, AS THE MANNER OF SOME IS, BUT EXORTING ONE ANOTHER, AND SO MUCH THE MORE AS YE SEE THE DAY APPROACHING.

Children of God are the sanctified or just men made perfect who shall continue to assemble in the name of the lord till the coming of the lord.

God has given him the name Jesus Christ, which is above all names and made him to be the father of Christendom, that all shall assemble in his name in one as Christians. To him alone God has made manifest the mystery of fellowship that men should understand the purpose of God in fellowship and to the intent that powers above and below should know the wisdom of God when the church gather unto Jesus Christ.

EPHESIANS 3:9-11

"AND TO MAKE ALL MEN SEE WHAT IS FELLOWSHIP OF THE MYSTERY, WHICH FROM THE BEGGINING OF THE WORLD HAD BEEN HID IN GOD, WHO CREATED ALL THINGS BY JESUS CHRIST.

TO THE INTENT THAT NOW UNTO THE PRINCIPALITIES, AND POWERS IN HEAVENLY PLACES, MIGHT BE KNOWN BY THE CHURCH, THE MANIFEST WISDOM OF GOD.

ACCORDING TO THE ETERNAL PURPOSE, WHICH HE HAS PURPOSED IN CHRIST JESUS OUR LORD.

Our Lord said, where two or three are gathered in his name, his presence is there, and in all he is omnipotent, omniscience and omnipresence. He is sufficient in all potentials, in power, in anointing, in signs and wonders. So when we gather together in the name of our Lord in a common accord, he will bestow upon us a union of anointing and multiplication of powers which is sufficient to pull down the strong holds of the adversary. The divine law of God has decreed it that when two sanctified individuals agree together as to touch anything in the name of our Lord Jesus Christ, that which they ask shall be done for them. Therefore when children of God gather together in the name of the Lord, the omnipotent God will be on their side. For the fact that this is the era of fuel and fire, the era of our lord Jesus Christ, God will kindle the fire of the Holy Spirit, against the powers of darkness, and the fire of the Holy Spirit will burn ablaze every spirit of error, and become a shield upon the children of God. Our gathering together unto the Lord is obviously a spiritual warfare against principalities and powers. That is the reason why we must be in the spirit for our prayer to ignite the power of the Holy Spirit.

ISAIAH 9:5-6

"FOR EVERY BATTLE OF THE WARRIOR IS WITH CONFUSED NOISE, AND GARMENTS ROLLED IN BLOOD, BUT THESE SHALL BE WITH BURNING AND FUEL OF FIRE. FOR UNTO US A CHILD IS BORN, UNTO US A SON IS GIVEN, AND THE GOVERNMENT SHALL BE UPON HIS SHOULDERS, AND HIS NAME SHALL BE CALLED WONDERFUL, COUNCILLOR, THE MIGHTY GOD, THE EVERLASTING FATHER, THE PRINCE OF PEACE.

As new born babes of God, the born again, we gather unto the lord of host, the God of peace, in one mind and spirit. We are in bond to obey all doctrine of Jesus Christ in good conscience, sharing all things in sanctification of spirit to the glory of God and truly believing in his exceeding greatness and powers.

EPHESIANS 1:19

"AND WHAT IS THE EXCEEDING GREATNESS OF HIS POWER, TO US WARD WHO BELIEVE ACCORDING TO THE WORKING OF HIS MIGHTY POWER.

THE COVENANT OF
KEEP WALKING

EPHESIANS 14:15

"AND THE LORD SAID UNTO MOSES, WHEREFORE CRIEST THOU UNTO ME.

SPEAK UNTO THE CHILDREN OF ISREAL THAT THEY GO FORWARD.

There are two seeds to sow and two seeds to harvest, in every life of mankind. These are the seed of eternal life, and eternal destruction. Each of these seeds when planted resurrects its nature. It is obvious that each of these seeds must die before regeneration of its kind, either eternal life or eternal death. Every man's conscience has two grounds to sow his seeds, and at the end, the harvest justifies the means. If you sow in the spirit you have sown in a divine ground for our lord Jesus, the way to the divine kingdom of God. And if you sow otherwise, you have sowed in the flesh, the runway of Satan to hell. The two destinations of life are identified by its movement. The movement to the kingdom of God is by walking to it, because it is a long journey through the wilderness. Then the movement to the pit of hell is by running to it, because it is in the fast lane. This is why God called Abraham to separate himself and walk in a perfect step with him.

GENESIS 17:1

"AND WHEN ABRAHAM WAS NINETY YEARS OLD AND NINE, THE LORD APPEARED TO ABRAM, AND SAID UNTO HIM,

I AM THE ALMIGHTY GOD, WALK BEFORE ME, AND BE THOU PERFECT.

Likewise, when Satan want to run away with his convert to the pit of hell, he will show them the beauty of the world, and the broad way that lead to it, and promise them the treasure of the earth and the glory of it. But be wise and have understanding because all that glitters are not gold. Our lord said to Judas Iscariot "That you are to do, do it quick". The ministry of Judas Iscariot is in the fast lane that is why he ended his ministry too quick.

PROVERBS 16:25

"THERE IS A WAY THAT SEEMETH RIGHT UNTO A MAN, BUT THE END THEREOF IS THE WAY OF DEATH.

God made a covenant with Abraham to keep walking perfect with him in spite of hindrance along the way. Jesus came and renewed the covenant of keep walking for the children of God. The covenant of Jesus Christ to the children of God is the covenant of determination and courage to keep walking in the name of the lord to possess the gate of our lord's promise. We must keep walking in the will of the father in his pace, timing and direction. Those that truly have decided to walk with God must have a perfect step. They must be obedient and faithful in all precepts and laws of God with the virtue of patience and long suffering. Those who refuse to walk in the perfect step of God in the wilderness to the promise land, they were possessed by the spirit of annoyance, complain and murmuring, and by so doing provoked the wrath of God, upon themselves, whereby they were consumed by fire and fiery serpent.

HEBREWS 3:7-11

"WHEREFORE AS THE HOLY GHOST SAITH, TODAY, IF YE WILL HEAR HIS VOICE,

HARDEN NOT YOUR HEARTS AS IN THE PROVOCATION, IN THE DAY OF TEMPTATION IN THE WILDERNESS,

WHEN YOUR FATHERS TEMPTED ME, PROVED ME, AND SAW MY WORKS FORTY YEARS.

WHEREFORE I WAS GREIVED WITH THAT GENERATION, AND SAID THEY HAVE NOT KNOWN MY WAYS.

SO I SWARE IN MY WRATH, THEY SHALL NOT ENTER INTO MY REST.

IN YOUR PATIENCE POSSESS YOUR SOUL

JAMES 5:7

"BE PATIENT BRETHREN THEREFORE UNTO THE COMING OF THE LORD, BEHOLD THE HUSBANDMAN WAITETH FOR THE PRECIOUS FRUIT OF THE EARTH, AND HATH LONG PATIENCE FOR IT, UNTIL HE RECEIVED THE EARLY AND LATTER RAIN.

The eternal weight of glory and the crown for the price of righteousness awaits those who endure forever in the kingdom race. It cannot be compared to the satanic affliction of the flesh and the tribulation that accompany our wilderness. If we understand that our journey to the kingdom of God is a matter of long suffering, then we will come to a compromise that it is a case of long patience. Jesus warned us that the world will hate us, and will come against us for his sake, but if we persevere in this tribulation, our patience shall not be in vain. We have a high calling and a promise that the end of it is eternal glory. So for a good reason it is a wise decision to obey he who has called us a call of blessing, no matter how rough or difficult the road to eternal life may be, though it is narrow road with a cross on the shoulder. The enemies may hinder but your God will give you victory, only move on to the righteous side with God.

ROMANS 2:7

"TO THEM WHOM BY PATIENT CONTINUANCE IN WELL DOING SEEK FOR GLORY, AND HONOR AND IMMORTALIY, ETERNAL LIFE.

No matter how long our God may tarry, his second mission must be accomplished. This is according to the testimony of his mission, which is the spirit of prophesy. Every prophesy about Jesus points at his first and second coming, which today the first has been fulfilled. Knowing that the word of God is truth, we confidently wait for his second mission, which is certain. But this we must wait patiently, faithfully steadfastly and confidently, without being weary or faint, but waiting in grace of his glory.

HABAKKUK 2:3

"FOR THE VISION IS YET FOR AN APPOINTED TIME, BUT AT THE END IT SHALL SPEAK AND NOT LIE, THOUGH IT TARRY, WAIT FOR IT, BECAUSE IT WILL SURELY COME, IT WILL NOT TARRY.

LIVING BY HIS COVENANT

GENESIS 17:7

"AND I WILL ESTABLISH MY COVENANT BETWEEEN ME AND THY SEED AFTER THEE IN THEIR GENERATIONS FOR ALL THEIR EVERLASTING COVENANT TO BE A GOD UNTO THEE AND TO THY SEED AFTER THEE.

Every intervention of God in our life is an intention to establish a divine relationship with us. After man lost his divine authority and dominion over things of the earth because of sin, everything that God created became his enemy. The sea became desirous to swallow man, the animals hunger to devour man, and the earth rejoice, ever hungry to feed with dead bodies of man. By the infinite mercies of God, he lifted up his countenance against man by establishing his first covenant with Noah to save man from further destruction. He commanded the flood to dry and the seas to flow to their bases, and the earth to be a place of inhabitation for man.

GENESIS 9:11-13

"AND I WILL ESTABLISH MY COVENANT WITH YOU, NEITHER SHALL ALL FLESH BE CUT OF ANYMORE, BY THE WATERS OF THE FLOOD, NEITHER SHALL THEIR ANYMORE BE A FLOOD TO DESTROY THE EARTH.

AND GOD SAID, THIS IS THE TOKEN OF THE COVENANT, WHICH I MAKE BETWEEN ME AND YOU AND EVERY LIVING CREATURE THAT IS WITH YOU, FOR PERPETUAL GENERATIONS. I DO SET MY BOW IN THE CLOUD AND IT SHALL BE FOR A TOKEN OF THE COVENANT BETWEEN ME AND THE EARTH.

Noah and his family lived by the covenant by believing in every word that God said to him. To achieve a perpetual generation, God proceeded by separating Abraham from his people for a covenant of the chosen. As a man of divine heart, Abraham willingly answered the calling of God. And God wanting to test his faith tempted Abraham by asking him to sacrifice his son Isaac for a burnt offering. Abraham the faithful servant of God beat God's imagination by attempting to sacrifice Isaac his only son according to God's word. God was overwhelmed by his faithfulness, and for this reason, he offered his only son for a perfect covenant. Abraham and his son lived by this covenant as the chosen one of God.

HEBREW 11:17

"BY FAITH ABRAHAM, WHEN HE WAS TRIED, OFFFERED UP ISAAC, AND HE THAT HAS RECEIVED THE PROMISES OFFERED UP HIS ONLY BEGOTTEN SON.

By Abraham's faith God became convinced of the faithfulness of man, he decided to bring man out of his miserable bondage. God set up the third covenant which is the covenant of the people; this includes the Jews and the gentiles. God this time made his son the chosen lamb for the sacrifice to take the place of Isaac for a final and perfect covenant. This covenant represents the covenant of light and glory of the Jews and gentiles.

ISAIAH 42:6-8

"I THE LORD HAVE CALLED THEE IN RIGHTEOUSNESS, AND WILL HOLD THY HAND,

AND WILL KEEP THEE AND GIVE THEE FOR A COVENANT OF THINE PEOPLE FOR A LIGHT OF THE GENTILES.

TO OPEN THE BLIND EYES, TO BRING OUT PRISONERS FROM THE PRISON, AND THEM THAT SIT IN DARKNESS OUT OF THE PRISON HOUSE.

I AM THE LORD THAT IS MY NAME AND GLORY, WILL I NOT GIVE TO ANOTHER NEITHER MY PRAISE TO GRAVEN IMAGES.

The sacrifice of this covenant was performed on the cross of Calvary which the son of God Jesus Christ of Nazareth was used as the lamb of sacrifice. It is called the new covenant in the blood of Jesus, the precious cleansing blood of Jesus, which took away the sins of the people.

MATTHEW 26:28

"FOR THIS IS MY BLOOD OF THE TESTAMENT, WHICH IS SHED FOR MANY FOR THE REMISSIONOF SINS.

Our God expects all children of God to live by the new covenant as the children of the perfect covenant. The covenant of the people is the covenant of light. This is the covenant that destroys the covenant of the old creature and transformed us into new creatures of the marvelous light. Living by this covenant is living in the light and walking in the light with Jesus. It is the covenant of no hiding place for the evil, where the light of Jesus made manifest all the hidden thing of the dark. This is not a covenant written on a table of stones but one written in our hearts.

HEBREW 8:10

"FOR THIS IS THE COVENANT THAT I WILL MAKE WITH THE HOUSE OF ISREAL AFTER THOSE DAYS, SAITH THE LORD. I WILL PUT MY LAWS INTO THEIR MINDS, AND WRITE THEM IN THEIR

*HEARTS. AND I WILL BE TO THEM A GOD, AND
THEY SHALL BE TO ME A PEOPLE.*

By this covenant God expects the children of God to serve him in spirit
and in truth that comes from the conscience of a man. It is the covenant of
righteousness in the heart of a man that yields the fruit of the Holy Spirit.

LIVING BY HIS WORD

LUKE 11:27-28

"AND IT CAME TO PASS, AS HE SPAKE THIS THINGS, A CERTAIN WOMAN OF THE COMPANY LIFTED UP HER VOICE AND SAID UNTO HIM, BLESSED IS THE WOMB THAT SAVED THEE AND THE PAPS WHICH THOU HAST SUCKED, BUT HE SAID YEA RATHER, BLESSED ARE THEY THAT HEAR THE WORD OF GOD AND KEEP IT.

The will of God for our life is to obey his word, and live by it as a living word for the living people. By the word of God we were made, by his word, we were destroyed, and by the same word, the believers in Christ were rekindled into life again, living for the hope of his second coming. So today, the word of God became a compass that pilots our life. It is shadow cast around our life that we shall not run away from. His word is a lamp to our feet that direct us from trespasses. It is a light that shows a clear picture of our destination into life. To the understanding, those who honour the word of God, it is a word to obey and live. The word is the way, the truth and abundance of life.

JOHN14:6

"JESUS SAITH UNTO HIM, I AM THE WAY, THE TRUTH AND THE LIFE. NO MAN COSMETH UNTO THE FATHER BUT BY ME.

Every soul desire to rest in the paradise of God, but not every spirit of man obeys the word of God, why? Because of evil compromise by the flesh of man. God expects the spirit of man to be the key player of our life. The life of a soul depends on the spirit, if the spirit guides the soul from evil destruction. It is in the spirit that God plants his words and expects it to bear fruit. This is possible if our spirit is in subjection to the power of the Holy Spirit. The spirit that is controlled by the flesh will certainly disobey God's word because it is under the custody of the flesh. Disobedience to God's word is agreement with the world which is in tune with the call of the flesh, lust of the eyes, and pride of life, and this is the quality of a soul in the pit of hell.

1 JOHN 2:16

"FOR ALL THAT IS IN THE WORLD, THE LUST OF THE FLESH AND THE LUST OF THE EYES, AND THE PRIDE OF LIFE, IS NOT OF THE FATHER BUT IS OF THE WORLD.

The assurance of a perfect life is to abide by the word of God. Obeying every letter of the word is walking in perfection with God, and declaring everlasting love for the infinite God. God's word is an entrance to God's love in our life. So those who obey the word of God dwell in the light which overcome the total darkness and the truth of God abide in them.

1 JOHN 2:4-6

"HE THAT SAITH I KNOW HIM, AND KEEPETH NOT HIS COMMANDMENTS, IS A LAIR, AND THE TRUTH IS NOT IN HIM.

BUT WHOSO KEEPETH HIS WORD, IN HIM VERILY IS THE WORD OF GOD PEFECTED, HEREBY KNOW WE THAT WE ARE IN HIM.

HE THAT SAITH HE ABIDETH IN HIM OUGHT HIMSELF ALSO TO WALK, EVEN AS HE WALKED.

Walking in perfection with God just as Abraham did is to keep the word of God in faith. Believing and trusting in every word that proceed out of God's mouth is wisdom of glory. The word is Christ, if we abide in the word in total obedience, the word will magnify Christ in our life. God expects his word to bear good fruit in us which obviously is a manifest of virtues of God, love, peace in righteousness.

JOHN 14:23

"IF A MAN LOVES ME, HE WILL KEEP MY WORD, AND MY FATHER WILL LOVE HIM, AND WE WILL COME UNTO HIM AND MAKE ABODE WITH HIM.

WALKING IN THE LIGHT OF JESUS

MATTHEW 5:14-16

"YE ARE THE LIGHT OF THE WORD, A CITY THAT IS SET ON AN HILL CANNOT BE HID, NEITHER DO MEN LIGHT A CANDLE AND PUT IT UNDER A BUSHEL, BUT ON A CANDLE STICK, AND IT GIVETH LIGHT TO ALL THAT ARE IN THE HOUSE. LET YOUR LIGHT SO SHINE BEFORE MEN SO THAT THEY CAN SEE YOUR GOOD WORKS, AND GLORIFY YOUR FATHER WHICH IS IN HEAVEN.

It is a great thing to serve Jesus and walk in his light. Jesus did three great miracles to bless the life of every believer.

A. he redeemed us from the life of death to the life of the living
B. he transformed us from darkness into his marvellous light
C. And translated us to his father's kingdom.

Since then, Christ expects all children of God to walk and shine in the light of God forever. The central truth to the children of God is to live in the light of God and to forsake all manners of sin. Sin is the habitual life of people in darkness. To be absolutely connected to the light of Jesus is to abide to the source of the marvellous light which is Jesus. To fellowship with him in sanctification of the spirit, and in earnest of obedience to the word of God. For us to keep walking in the light, we must passionately hate evil and love the good. If we serve God and still involve ourselves in the practice of things of the darkness definitely our activities will manifest in the light. It is no hiding place for transgressors.

EPHESIANS 5:8-13

"FOR YE WERE SOMETIMES DARKNESS, BUT NOW ARE YE LIGHT IN THE LORD, WALK AS CHILDREN OF LIGHT.

FOR THE FRUIT OF THE SPIRIT IS IN ALL GOODNESS AND RIGHTOUSNESS AND TRUTH.

PROVING WHAT IS ACCEPTABLE UNTO THE LORD, AND HAVING NO FELLOWSHIP WITH THE UNFRUITFUL WORKS OF DARKNESS, BUT RATHER REPROVE THEM FOR IT IS A SHAME TO SPEAK OF THOSE THINGS THAT ARE REPROVED AND MADE MANIFEST BY THE LIGHT. FOR WHOSEOVER MADE MANIFEST IS OF THE LIGHT.

We serve the God of light and in him there is no darkness, and to be the children of God we must shine in the light of God, in spirit, soul and body. To be in the light is to follow the way of righteousness, and to be righteous is to obey the instructions of the Holy Spirit, which will lead us to serve God in clear conscience. This simply means to cleave to that which is good and abhor that which is evil, falling in love with that which leads to life, and hatred to that that leads to death, such as the work of the flesh.

GALATIANS 5:19-21

"NOW THE WORK OF THE FLESH ARE MANIFEST WHICH ARE THESE; ADULTERY, FORNICATION, UNCLEANLINESS, LASCIVIOUSNESS, IDOLATERY, STRIFE, SEDITIONS, HERESIES, ENVYING, MURDERS, DRUNKENESS, REVELLINGS, AND SUCH LIKE OF WHICH I TELL YOU BEFORE AS

I HAVE ALSO TOLD YOU IN TIME PAST, THAT WHICH THEY DO SUCH THINGS SHALL NOT INHERIT THE KINGDOM OF GOD.

Those that are living in the light they walk in the spirit, and things of light and spirit manifest in glory and in power through our lord Jesus in our life. All that walk in the light they are the circumcisions that fellowship in spirit with our lord. In this manner, the activities of the light cannot be made manifest in the darkness, but the things of the darkness is made manifest in the light because darkness cannot comprehend the things of the light of Jesus.

Light and darkness are contrary to one another, they are enemies unto eternity. It is impossible to fellowship with Christ and at the same time associate with devil. There will be a mixed reaction and the overall result will be absolutely negative. The citizens of light they aspire of the things above which is the source of light while the citizens of darkness think of things below which comes from the pit of hell, the bottomless pit.

1 JOHN 1:5-7

"THIS THEN IS THE MESSAGE, WHICH WE HAVE HEARD OF HIM, AND DECLARE UNTO YOU, THAT GOD IS LIGHT, AND IN HIM IS NO DARKNESS AT ALL.

IF WE SAY THAT WE HAVE FELLOWSHIP WITH HIM, AND WALK IN DARKNESS, WE LIE, AND DO NOT THE TRUTH. BUT IF WE WALK IN THE LIGHT, AS HE IS IN THE LIGHT, WE HAVE FELLOWSHIP WITH ONE WITH ANOTHER AND THE BLOOD OF JESUS CHRIST CLEANSETH US FROM ALL SIN.

LIVING IN THE GLORY OF GOD

1 CORINTHIANS 1:29-31

"THAT NO FLESH SHOULD GLORY IN HIS PRESENCE.

BUT OF HIM ARE YE IN CHRIST JESUS, WHO OF GOD IS MADE UNTO US WISDOM, AND RIGHTEOUSNESS, AND SANTIFICATION, AND REDEMPTION.

THAT ACCORDING AS IT IS WRITTEN, HE THAT GLORIETH, LET HIM GLORY IN THE LORD.

The glory of God is the beauty of God; the children of God are the beauty of God, so we are his glory. To give a practical illustration, Jesus is the vine, while the children of God are the branches. It is understood that the beauty of a branch is in its branches, because of the flowers and fruits. We are the branches that produce the beauty of God, so we are the glory of God. That is why God guide us jealously that we should not glory in any other god, but only in our lord Jesus Christ. Children of God are the image and glory of the God. God has declared that the former things has passed, but now, new things has taken over, he cannot share his glory with graven image.

ISAIAH 42:8-9

"I AM THE LORD, THAT IS MY NAME AND GLORY, WILL I NOT GIVE TO ANOTHER, NEITHER MY PRAISE TO GRAVEN IMAGE.

149

BEHOLD THE FORMER THINGS ARE COME TO PASS, AND NEW THINGS DO I DECLARE UNTO THEE, BEFORE THEY SPRING FORTH, I TELL YOU OF THEM.

Why we must live in the glory of God is because God lives in us, meaning that his glory is in us. Our body is the temple of God by all reason; it should magnify Christ and glorify God. There is no glory without Holiness. For the glory of God to manifest in a child of God, he or she must keep to absolute holiness, you must flee from all manners of sin, but rather inhabit in a holy environment. This is to permit the Holy Spirit which is the spirit of glory to glorify your body. You should be sanctified in body, soul and spirit, and represent a symbol of dews of glory.

1 CORINTHIANS 6:18-20

"FLEE FORNICATION, EVERY SIN THAT A MAN DOETH IS WITHOUT THE BODY, BUT HE THAT COMMITETH FORNICATION SIN AGAINST HIS BODY.

WHAT? KNOW YE NOT THAT YOUR BODY IS THE TEMPLE OF THE HOLY GHOST WHICH IS IN YOU, WHICH YE HAVE OF GOD AND YE ARE NOT YOUR OWN, FOR YE ARE BOUGHT WITH A PRICE, THEREFORE GLORIFY GOD WITH YOUR BODY, AND IN YOUR SPIRIT, WHICH ARE GODS.

Christ is the king of glory, all glory and honor is ascribed to him. He is the one that descended in glory to the land of the dead, and ascended in glory into heaven. If you are in Christ, his body is in you, and his glory is in you. God expects the children of God as the image of his glory to maintain and preserve his glory in them with much caution; that is by obeying the word of God as a guide to life. A glorious child of God will grow from glory to glory, if totally submitted to the spirit of the lord.

2 CORINTHIANS 3:17-18

"NOW THE LORD IS THAT SPIRIT, AND WHERE THE SPIRIT OF THE LORD IS, THERE IS LIBERTY. BUT WE ARE WITH OPEN FACE BEHOLD ALL WITH A GLASS THE GLORY OF THE LORD, ARE CHALLANGED INTO THE SAME IMAGE FROM GLORY TO GLORY, EVEN AS BY THE SPIRIT OF THE LORD.

MY FATHER'S HOUSE NOT THE DEN OF THIEVES

LUKE 19:45-46

"AND HE WENT INTO THE TEMPLE AND BEGAN TO CAST OUT THEM THAT SOLD THEREIN AND THEM THAT BOUGHT

SAYING UNTO THEM, IT IS WRITTEN, MY HOUSE IS THE HOUSE OF PRAYER, AND YE HAVE MADE IT TO A DEN OF THEIVES.

The temple of the almighty God is his habitual place, a place where the holy and perfect God indwell. It is established in glory, a seat of honour and power filled with his awesome presence, and as such, it should be a place where the children of God reverence with fear and trembling for the sake of his greatness and mightiness. But this adulterous generation as Jesus called them sees the house of God in different perspective; it is rather regarded as a house of merchandise than the holy house of God. Today, the get rich quick, the prosperity gospel preachers, those who work for their bellies as the bible described them has over taken the church of God for the wealth of the world. They have forsaken the suffering of Christ on the Cross of Calvary and turned to be the enemies of Christ.

PHILIPPIANS 3:18-19

"FOR MANY WORK FOR WHOM I HAVE TOLD YOU OFTEN, AND NOW TELL YOU EVEN WEEPING,

THAT THEY ARE THE ENEMIES OF THE CROSS OF CHRIST.

WHOSE END IS DESTRUCTION, WHOSE GOD IS THEIR BELLY, AND WHOSE GLORY IS IN THEIR SHAME, WHO MIND EARTHLY THINGS.

Jesus warned us of covetousness, to be careful not to allow the treasure of the earth to over rule our affections of things above. The word of God said, seek ye first the kingdom of God, and his righteousness and all this things shall be added unto you. Children of God should be curious seekers of Christ and the kingdom of God and not conscious seekers of material gain in the house of God. The house of God should be a place of gain for the incorruptible minds who serve God in truth and in spirit for righteousness sake. It should not be a hiding place for rubbers who has converted the house of God to a money making house or financial investment house. The bible made it clear that the corrupt mind will have their soul tortured in hell fire. Wisdom is the principal thing, set your mind on the thing above and you will possess your soul in the devine kingdom of God.

LUKE 12:15

"AND HE SAID UNTO THEM, TAKE HEED AND BEWARE OF COVETOUSNESS FOR A MAN'S LIFE CONSISTETH NOT IN THE ABUNDANCE OF THINGS WHICH HE POSSESSED.

Money as the bible said is the root of evil, we should be careful not to allow the devil influence in money to derail the purpose by which he has called us. Ministers of God should feed the flocks of God and not to plant them as money yielding tree and taking undue advantage of their income and wealth, but to work for God in honesty and with good conscience, God is a rewarder of them that diligently seek him.

1 PETER 5:2-3

"FEED THE FLOCK OF GOD WHICH IS AMONG YOU, TAKING THE OVER SIGHT THEREOF, NOT BY CONSTRAINT BUT WILLINGLY, NOT OF FILTHY LUCRE, BUT OF A READY MIND.

NEITHER AS BEING LORD OUR GOD'S HERITAGE, BUT BEING EXAMPLE OF THE FLOCK.

1 TIMOTHY 6:10-11

"FOR THE LOVE OF MONEY IS THE ROOT OF ALL EVIL, WHICH WHILE SOME COVETED AFTER, THEY HAVE ERRED FROM THE FAITH AND PIERCED THEMSELVES THROUGH WITH MANY SORROWS.

BUT THOU O MAN OF GOD FLEE THESE THINGS, BUT FOLLOW AFTER RIGHTOUSNESS, GODLINESS, FAITH, LOVE, PATIENCE, MEEKNESS.

BE NOT UNWISE; BEWARE OF THE WORKS OF ANCIENT MYSTERY

EPHESIANS 5:14-15

WHERFORE HE SAITH, AWAKE THOU THAT SLEEPEST, AND ARISE FROM THE DEAD, AND CHRIST SHALL GIVE THEE LIGHT.

SO THEN THAT YE WALK CIRCUMSPECTLY, NOT AS FOOLS, BUT AS WISE.

REDEEMING THE TIME BECAUSE THE DAYS ARE EVIL.

By their fruits we shall know them, they are known by the unfruitful works of the darkness, works of flesh and of the world. They are the true colours of ancient Babylon and Egyptian secret magic foundation, channels of deception, delusion and apostasy of the time. All for the purpose of derailing souls from the truth and light, and misleading them to the pit of darkness. Hypocrites in nature with evil trade mark; they are wolves in sheep clothing.

2 CORINTHIANS 11:13-15

"FOR SUCH ARE FALSE PROPHETS, DECIETFUL WORKERS, TRANSFORMING THEMSELVES INTO THE APOSTLES OF CHRIST.

AND NO MARVEL, FOR SATAN HIMSELF IS TRANSFORMED INTO AN ANGEL OF LIGHT. THEREFORE, IT IS NO GREAT THING IF MINISTERS BE TRANSFORMED AS THE MINISTERS OF RIGHTEOUSNESS WHO'S ENDS SHALL BE ACCORDING TO THEIR WORKS.

These are co-workers of Anti-Christ, who preach and teach heresy. The mundane Christian preachers who have their scheme of luring innocent people into the worship of the devil by their subtle way of propagating prosperity gospel rather than preaching the power of Calvary, which is the open door to salvation of Christ. You can identify them by their nature; they are as wise as serpent. Righteous in the day and evil in the dark; they are called the white sepulchers.

These groups are known by their spirit, they are the manifest workers of iniquity. They are spectacular and popular in two magic abilities; the ability to pull large crowd under spell bond, and the ability to perform evil miracles with the spirit of apostasy. Be careful for whatever that is in the dark shall be brought to light. What is hidden shall be revealed and made manifest in the open.

2 THESSALONIANS 2:7-9

"FOR THE MISTERY OF INIQUITY DOTH READY WORK, ONLY HE WHO NOW LETETH WILL LET, UNTIL HE BE TAKEN OUT OF THE WAY.

AND THEN SHALL THAT WICKED BE REVEALED WHOM THE LORD SHALL CONSUME WITH THE SPIRIT OF HIS MOUTH, AND SHALL DESTROY WITH THE BRIGHTNESS OF HIS COMING.

EVEN HIM WHOSE COMING IS AFTER THE WORK OF SATAN WITH ALL POWERS AND SIGNS AND LYING WONDERS.

DESTITUTE OF THE TRUTH
AND OF THE WORD

1 TIMOTHY 6:3-5

"IF ANY MAN TEACH OTHERWISE, AND CONSENT NOT TO WHOLESOME WORDS, EVEN THE WORD OF OUR LORD JESUS CHRIST, AND TO THE DOCTRINE WHICH IS ACCORDING TO GODLINESS.

HE IS PROUD, KNOWING NOTHING, BUT DOTING ABOUT QUESTIONS, AND STIFES OF WORDS, WHEREOF COMETH ENVY, STIFE, RAILINGS, EVIL SURMISING.

PERVERSE DISPUTING OF MEN OF CORRUPT MINDS, AND DESTITUTE OF THE TRUTH, SUPPOSING THAT GAIN IS GODLINESS, FROM SUCH WITHDRAW THYSELF.

As Jannes and Jambres opposed Moses and the word of God, as Anathema Maranatha was an Anti-Christ. So also the people of this word opposed the word of God professing to be the master of the word, but inside out they are the mediocre of the word of God. The understanding of the word of light does not base on logical foundation or philosophical understanding, but the grace of the anointing of the spirit of the living God. The knowledge of the word of God is not by paragon of theological advancement, but a gift of the Holy Spirit and a special calling of God. The skill is not by acquiring knowledge or experience in the word, but a divine deposit of chariot of grace of understanding in the word of God, by auction of the Holy Spirit.

JOHN 3:34

"FOR HE WHOM GOD HATH SENT SPEAKETH THE WORD OF GOD, FOR GOD GIVETH NOT THE SPIRIT BY MEASURE UNTO HIM.

We have doctors and professors of the word of God who has acquired their skills through learning and understanding of the word in the flesh. This group believes in the power of learning and high degree of intellectualism, thereby erring in the word of God. Someone can advance in the word of God only if you submit your learning power to the teaching of the Holy Spirit, who will open the entrance of the word of God to your understanding. Our God has chosen to give it to them that are poor in spirit, for the kingdom of God belongs to them, why because they are humble in spirit, and are ready to learn and understand the word of God.

MATTHEW 11:25-26

"AT THAT TIME, JESUS ANSWERED AND SAID, I THANK THEE, O FATHER, LORD OF HEAVEN AND EARTH, BECAUSE THOU HATH HID THESE THINGS FROM THE WISE AND PRUDENT AND HATH REVEALED THEM UNTO BABIES.

EVEN SO FATHER, FOR SO IT SEEMED GOOD IN THY SIGHT.

Today, multitude of people of the world believe that God the son did not come in flesh to die for the sin of the world, and that he did not rise and ascend to heaven to give us eternal life. Instead their opinion is that Jesus is the son of man and not the son of God. Because of this ignorance and empty pride, they deny themselves the right to salvation of Christ and they remained in blind of the gospel of light, and their light darkened.

ROMANS 1:20-22

FOR THE INVISIBLE THINGS OF HIM FROM THE CREATION OF THE WORLD ARE CLEARLY SEEN, BEING UNDERSTOOD BY THE THINGS THAT ARE MADE, EVEN HIS ETERNAL POWER AND HIS ETERNAL POWER AND GOD HEAD, SO THAT THEY ARE WITHOUT EXCUSE.

BECAUSE THAT WHEN THEY KNOW GOD, THEY GLORIFY HIM NOT AS GOD NEITHER WERE THANKFUL, BUT BECAME VAIN IN THEIR IMAGINATIONS, AND THEIR FOOLISH HEARTS WHERE DARKENED.

The bible describes such people as Godless, men of corrupt minds, ever learning but not able to come to the knowledge of truth, from such people run away, they have no God.

2 JOHN 1:9-16

"WHOEVER TRANSGRESSETH AND ABIDETH NOT IN THE DOCTRINE OF CHRIST HATH NOT GOD. HE THAT ABIDETH IN THE DOCTRINE OF CHRIST, HE HATH BOTH THE FATHER AND THE SON.

IF THERE COME ANY UNTO YOU, AND BRING NOT THESE DOCTRINE, RECEIVE HIM NOT INTO YOUR HOUSE, NEITHER BID HIM GOD SPEED.

PUTTING CHRIST TO AN OPEN SHAME

HEBREW 6:4-6

"FOR IT IS IMPOSSIBLE FOR THOSE WHO WERE ONCE ENLIGTENED, AND HAVE TASTED OF THE HEAVENLY GIFT, AND WHERE MADE PARTAKERS OF THE HOLY GHOST.

AND HAVE TASTED THE GOOD WORD OF THE LORD, AND THE POWERS OF THE LORD TO COME.

IF THEY SHALL FALL AWAY, TO RENEW THEM AGAIN UNTO REPENTANCE, SEEING THEY CRUSIFY TO THEMSELVES UNTO THE SON OF GOD AFRESH, AND PUT HIM TO AN OPEN SHAME.

Christ being crucified on the cross, has brought a crown of honour, and glory to the children of God, from the mud of shame to glory, from Adam's cage to the freedom of Jesus Christ. Christ is the horn of salvation and as well the well of salvation. He is the one that announces our salvation, and the one that draws those that believe in him from the deep sea of the devil to the well of salvation, the life giving water of the Holy Spirit. Christ our saviour saved us in four cardinal ways to bring us to his divine nature;

1. Withdrawing us from the shadow of death.
2. Withdrawing us from the pit of hell.
3. Saving us from the cloud of the evil.

4. Bringing us out of the iniquities of the world.

Then he ushered us into his glorious attributes;

1. Into his marvellous light.
2. Into the glorious nature of God
3. Into his holiness.
4. Into his victorious nature.
5. Into his blessedness.

This is the sacrifice he made to keep your life precious in the holy hands of God. He died for us publicly to remove our shame and it shall be wise to accept openly that he died that we might be renewed into life.

1 TIMOTHY 1:15

"THIS IS A FAITHFUL SAYING AND WORTHY OF ALL ACCEPTATIONS THAT CHRIST JESUS CAME TO SAVE SINNERS OF WHOM I AM CHIEF.

Knowing he has done this for you, it will be grievous if we that has believed and is saved should withdraw again into the world, as Demas did withdraw into the world, and this will amount to crucifying Christ a second time. Going back to what we have rejected and making it a normal habit is the pig's nature. Should Christ redeem be like a pig? The word of God said in the book of Ezekiel 18, 24, that the glory will not be remembered. The redeemed should not be compared with the dog who goes back to its vomit. If you have been transformed into the light of Jesus you have no excuse again to be overshadowed by the cloud of darkness, because that will mean grieving the Holy Spirit of redemption.

2 PETER 2:20-22

"FOR IF AFTER THEY HAVE ESCAPED THE POLLUTION OF THE WORLD THROUGH THE KNOWLEDGE OF THE LORD AND SAVIOR JESUS CHRIST, THEY ARE AGAIN ENTANGLED THEREIN,

AND OVERCOME, AND LATTER END IS WORSE WITH THEM THAN THE BEGINNING.

FOR IT WAS BETTER FOR THEM NOT TO HAVE KNOWN THE WAGE OF RIGHTEOUSNESS THAN AFTER THEY HAVE KNOWN IT TO TURN FROM THE HOLY COMMANDMENT DELIVERED UNTO THEM.

BUT IT IS HAPPENED UNTO THEM ACCORDING TO THE TRUE PROVERB. THE DOG TURNED TO HIS OWN VOMIT AGAIN AND SOW THAT WAS WASHED TO WALLOWING IN THE MIRE.

ENEMIES OF THE CROSS OF CHRIST

PHILIPPIANS 3:18-19

"FOR MANY WALK OF WHOM I HAVE TOLD YOU OFTEN AND NOW TELL YOU EVEN WEEPING, THAT THEY ARE THE ENEMIES OF THE CROSS OF CHRIST.

WHOSE END IS DESTRUCTION, WHOSE GOD IS THEIR BELLY, AND WHOSE GLORY IS IN THEIR SHAME, WHOSE MIND EARTHLY THINGS.

As Anathema Marantha love not Jesus and as Jannes and Jambres withhold the world of God so also this ungodly generation oppose the word of light and has made themselves the enemies of Christ. For Christ has died on the cross once and will not die the second time for any reason or excuse. If you are not gathering with him you are scattering and has made yourself the enemy of Christ. His word in the book of proverbs 8:17, says, *"I LOVE HIM THAT LOVE ME, AND THOSE THAT SEEK ME EARLY SHALL FIND ME, BUT HE THAT SINNETH AGAINST ME WRONGETH HIS OWN SOUL, ALL THEY THAT HATE ME LOVE DEATH.*

Jesus has given us the verdict of his own Judgment against his enemies, those that hate him shall die eternal death. Those that turn the truth about Christ into lies shall receive their wages in hell fire, which is the portion of the wicked.

2 PETER 2:12-13

"BUT THESE ARE NATURAL BRUTE BEASTS MADE TO BE TAKEN AND DESTROYED, SPEAK EVIL OF THE THINGS THAT THEY UNDERSTAND NOT AND SHALL UTTERLY PERISH IN THEIR OWN CORRUPTION.

AND SHALL RECEIVE THE REWARD OF UNRIGHTEOUSNESS, AS THEY THAT COUNT IT PLEASURE TO RIOT IN THE DAY. SPOTS THEY ARE AND BLEMISHES, SPOTING THEMSELVES WITH THEIR OWN DECIEVINGS WHILE THEY FEAST WITH YOU.

Like Hymeneaus and Philetus who erred in the truth of the gospel of Christ and also deceived others to fall out of the faith. This is how many in this end time has become evil preachers of the word, people without conscience who has turned the word of God into a merchandise to fulfil their own purpose, lovers of pleasure and earthly gain. Without shame, they have turned Christianity into a modern fashion doing those things that are not convenient in the sight of God, men wearing ear rings and plating their hairs as women, and also the women wearing men's wears, as well leaving their hair uncovered in the church of God.

2 PETER 2:2-3

"AND MANY SHALL FOLLOW THEIR PENICIOUS WAYS, BY REASON OF WHOM THE WAY OF THE TRUTH SHALL EVIL BE SPOKEN OF

AND THROUGH COVETIOUSNESS SHALL THEY WITH FEIGNED WORDS MAKE MARCHANDISE OF YOU, WHOSE JUDGEMENT NOW OF A LONG TIME LINGER NOT, AND THEIR DAMNATION SLUMBERETH NOT.

WORK OUT YOUR SALVATION WITH FEAR AND TREMBLING

PHILIPPIANS 2:12

"WHEREFORE MY BELOVED AS YE HAS ALWAYS OBEYED, NOT AS IN MY PRESENCE ONLY, BUT NOW MUCH MORE IN MY ABSENCE, WORK OUT YOUR OWN SALVATION WITH FEAR AND TREMBLING.

FOR IT IS GOD WHO WORKETH IN YOU, BOTH TO WILL AND TO DO OF HIS GOOD PLEASURE.

Life without the wisdom of God is life with disastrous end. Therefore wisdom is the principle thing about life, and to be in good direction, the beginning of wisdom is the fear of God. If we know where we are coming from, and where we are going to, we will know that someone supernatural owns the life we live, and that he has a purpose for creating our life. Then we should imagine how terrible it will be for us to live the negative way from his plan for our life. The bible said it is a fearful thing for us to fall into the hands of the living God. Our God is a consuming fire, and every soul that sin he shall throw into the lake of fire.

HEBREW 12:28-29

"WHEREFORE WE RECEIVE A KINGDOM WHICH CANNOT BE MOVED, LET US HAVE GRACE, WHEREBY WE MAY SERVE GOD, ACCEPTABLE WITH REVERENCE AND WITH GODLY FEAR.

FOR OUR GOD IS A CONSUMING FIRE.

God is the judge of all things on earth and in heaven, He is the destiny of our fate in life or in death, he predestines the journey of our life, he owns the soul of our life and determines where it settles, whether in hell or in heaven. He is a just God and he judges according to the laws and precepts of his kingdom. His laws are holy and his precepts are righteous. Our God expects us to abide by the commandments of his laws and precepts, in order to inherit his kingdom. It is his pleasure that we should inherit his kingdom, but if we go contrary to his words, then we become disobedient to him, and the wages of disobedience to God is eternal death in hell fire. The bible said fear God for he alone can kill and throw into the lake of fire.

LUKE 12:4-5

"AND I SAY UNTO YOU MY FRIENDS, BE NOT AFRAID OF THEM THAT KILL THE BODY, AND AFTER THAT HAVE NO MORE THAT THEY CAN DO.

BUT I WILL FORE WARN YOU WHO YOU SHALL FEAR, FEAR HIM WHICH AFTER HE HAS KILLED HAS THE POWER TO CAST INTO HELL, YEA, I SAY UNTO YOU FEAR HIM.

Our soul is owned by God the almighty, he is the bishop of our soul, and he expects our soul to come unto him undefiled. Our soul came from God in purity and should strive to abide in holiness of his origin. The soul is always the last man standing in the last day. The body will be separated from the spirit and the spirit will be separated from the soul. The soul will stand in the presence of God to defend himself of his works on earth. The soul that sinneth shall die and the soul which strives for righteousness shall live everlasting.

EZEKIEL 18:4

*"BEHOLD ALL SOULS ARE MINE, AS THE SOUL OF
THE FATHER, SO ALSO THE SOUL OF THE SON IS
MINE, THE SOUL THAT SINNETH IT SHALL DIE.*

READERS REFLECTION

LIFE IS ABOUT DIVINE ROYAL CROWN ON THE HEAD

A precious life is all about divine royal crown on the head. A good life starts with Jesus and end at lifting up of the royal crown in Christ victory. He who is deceived is still dwelling in the dark side. By virtue of Christ overflowing grace children of God who work good in the sight of God are entitled to Christ royal crown. Kingdom of God is not negotiable; it is a compulsory battle race to win a crown of life. Those who refuse to obey the rules will fall by the way side, and end up with the crown of damnation. By the grace of our Lord who made us the bonafide children of his father's kingdom we become kings and priests with a reward of a glorious crown. Christ's crown is the identity of children of divine heaven, those who enter the kingdom without the glorious crown are the gate crashers whose portion is brimstone and fire. Fulfilling all righteousness and abhorring the unrighteous is a certificate of merit to receive the royal crown.

REVELATION 3; 11

BEHOLD, I COME QUICKLY; HOLD THOU FAST WHICH THOU HAST, THAT NO MAN TAKE THY CROWN.

It is obvious that heaven bound children of God must have their victoriuos crown as an honour to the Lord who rewards us according to our work. What is worth doing is worth doing well. Start the race with

Jesus, be steadfast in the spirit, walk by his pace and certainly you will gain entrance through the flood gate of heaven which is the joy of the soul. No one in the kingdom of righteousness can serve God without casting down his crown before the throne that is why it is mandatory that we must strive in our spiritual drive to overcome the odds of this end time in other to receive our crown of life. We have a glorious invitation from the Lord, a wedding invitation and the dressing pattern permitted is the sanctified white robe and the royal crown of Christ. Jesus Christ is the only authority to certify the genius crown; in this case there is no manouver, we must go through his approval. In this manner of conversation a man of wisdom will make hay while the sun shines. Christ once wore the crown of thorns, the crown of anguish for you and me but when he ascended to heaven his father crowned him with the glorious crown. In this way Christ expects us to persevere in our anguish for his sake and move on to the righteous side to possess the victorious crown of life. Dear brethren leave your comfort zone; the world is a comfort zone. Abraham left his comfort zone to possess the promise land. Except you separate yourself from the world you will not have your portion in the kingdom of God. Life is a journey possessed by the power of spirit, either negative or positive spirit. You are either possessed by the spirit of Satan or the spirit of Jesus, to whom ye yield yourself a servant his servant ye are. Grace abounds if you yield a repentant heart and allow Christ to reign in your heart and his spirit taking a lead in your life, surely you will neither stumble nor fall. Those in mount Zion will not be removed because they stand upon the rock of ages [Christ] whose foundation is unshakeable. Life is not what you make of it but what life makes of you, you do not own life but life owns you. Christ is life and he owns your life, he died to redeem your life and he becomes the prince of your life and the bishop of your soul.

Darkness is for the blind and light is for them that have sight. Christ represents light and the generation of those that have light. The manifestation of the power of light comes from above while the manipulation of the things of darkness comes from the dark tunnel, the pit of the unrighteous spirit. Be careful what you wish, life is like a vapour, every one you see today will go some day, where is your pride? Ask yourself who is triumphing now? The world or Christ who has risen from death? The world is a market place whatever you buy you shall take home.

We are in a garden field; whatever you sow you will reap. Who is he that condemneth? Christ or the world?

ROMANS 8:34

WHO IS HE THAT CONDEMNETH? IT IS CHRIST THAT DIED, YEA RATHER, THAT IS RISEN AGAIN WHO IS EVEN AT THE RIGHT HAND OF GOD, WHO ALSO MAKETH INTERCESSION FOR US.

READERS REFLECTION

READERS REFLECTION

Printed in the United States
By Bookmasters